SAVE HALF, RETIRE FAST

Your Complete Guide to Financial Independence and Early Retirement From Money Mindset to Retired Millionaire

Frankie Calkins

Cover Design by Andy Layman
Edited by Nis Jose

www.TheMoneyResolution.com
frankie@themoneyresolution.com

Follow The Money Resolution on YouTube for personal finance videos weekly!

#SAVEHALFBOOK

Dedication

For my wife (and other half) Claire
You are my motivation and inspiration daily

In 2021, we got engaged, planned a wedding, got married, went on a honeymoon, and bought our first house during the pandemic in the process of writing this book over the course of 1 year.

A SPECIAL GIFT FOR YOU

SAVE MONEY RESOLUTION COURSE

Enjoy huge savings on my course to help you save your first (or next) $10,000 faster than you thought was possible.

You get 2.5 hours of video lessons, a 15 page workbook, a personalized one-sheet planner, slides, and lifetime access.

Get it 90% (!) off with code SAVEHALFBOOK
as a thank you for your purchase and support!

Learn more and claim your offer at:
www.TheMoneyResolution.com

Foreword

I Couldn't NOT Write This Book

In July 2020, I published my second book, Money, You Can Hack It. I had an epiphany that I was passionate about sharing with the world. I came to the realization that you can stop living paycheck to paycheck with a little DIY financial creativity.

Six months later in January of 2021, I told myself *I'm not writing a book this year*. Money, You Can Hack It took me more than 15 months to produce. It was exhausting and all-consuming. The book creation process is grueling. I needed a break. I fell in love with sharing finance tips and lessons on YouTube, so I committed to making 100 YouTube videos in 2021 instead.

On YouTube, I share videos twice a week. My goal with the channel has always been to help people get resolved to get good with money. I never considered it a FIRE movement (financial independence, retire early) channel, until somebody in the comments pointed out it kind of was and suggested I look into FIRE strategies.

After going down a research rabbit hole into the FIRE movement I discovered I believed in the same core values that FIRE-seekers follow. I realized that my mindset with money, investing strategies, and financial philosophy aligned with core FIRE values. I felt immense relief knowing there was an entire community of people that felt exactly how I felt about money. I was hooked. I was inspired. I now had a goal I never considered: retire early. I felt enlightened and incredibly motivated after committing to this newfound goal. I sought the financial freedom of no longer needing to trade my time for money, but instead, to be able to use that time to live my life to the fullest. In my continuous research I developed a deeper understanding of the technical side of money, and I bettered my relationship with money throughout the process.

In August 2020, I shared my first FIRE video: "The #1 Secret to Gain Financial Independence & Retire Early." From then on, I pivoted to focus almost exclusively on FIRE movement strategies. Halfway through 2021, roughly 50 published videos in, I realized that I could tie my videos ideas together and connect everything I have learned about early retirement to a bigger project: this book. Correction: I didn't realize I *could* do it. I realized I *must* do it.

It started as a spark of an idea but grew into an overwhelming desire. Once the seed was planted, I thought about making this book everyday. I couldn't *not* make it. I had to share this part of my journey and learnings. I wanted to help and inspire others the way I felt inspired. If nothing else, I needed to document this chapter of my life. It was time to get to work. I made a YouTube video announcing that I was writing a book. *"...and it will be out before the end of the year!"*, I declared. That was my way of holding myself accountable.

When I was finished recording that video I remember thinking *"Here we go again!"* I will never forget how excited I was for this book before you to be finished before I put a single word to paper. I quickly outlined 20 chapters to cover in around 150 pages. Clearly brevity is not my strong suit…

How do you write a book that is in your soul—a book that you're passionate about? One day at a time. One chapter at a time. Or in my case, one video twice a week for a year. Thank you for being a part of the coming chapters literally, and this chapter in my life figuratively. I hope this book suits you well to get you on the path and keeps you on the path to financial independence and early retirement.

This book is a snapshot in time so I will not pretend to know it all. I hope that makes it more relatable. I hope you find it easier to follow a guide that's only a few steps, or year ahead of you if you're just getting started. Nobody like a know-it-all anyways… I am an ordinary person who wants to live a an extraordinary life. If you are reading this, I suspect we have a lot in common. Let's do this together.

Writing a book is incredibly challenging but deeply rewarding,

Foreword

I Couldn't NOT Write This Book

In July 2020, I published my second book, Money, You Can Hack It. I had an epiphany that I was passionate about sharing with the world. I came to the realization that you can stop living paycheck to paycheck with a little DIY financial creativity.

Six months later in January of 2021, I told myself *I'm not writing a book this year*. Money, You Can Hack It took me more than 15 months to produce. It was exhausting and all-consuming. The book creation process is grueling. I needed a break. I fell in love with sharing finance tips and lessons on YouTube, so I committed to making 100 YouTube videos in 2021 instead.

On YouTube, I share videos twice a week. My goal with the channel has always been to help people get resolved to get good with money. I never considered it a FIRE movement (financial independence, retire early) channel, until somebody in the comments pointed out it kind of was and suggested I look into FIRE strategies.

After going down a research rabbit hole into the FIRE movement I discovered I believed in the same core values that FIRE-seekers follow. I realized that my mindset with money, investing strategies, and financial philosophy aligned with core FIRE values. I felt immense relief knowing there was an entire community of people that felt exactly how I felt about money. I was hooked. I was inspired. I now had a goal I never considered: retire early. I felt enlightened and incredibly motivated after committing to this newfound goal. I sought the financial freedom of no longer needing to trade my time for money, but instead, to be able to use that time to live my life to the fullest. In my continuous research I developed a deeper understanding of the technical side of money, and I bettered my relationship with money throughout the process.

In August 2020, I shared my first FIRE video: "The #1 Secret to Gain Financial Independence & Retire Early." From then on, I pivoted to focus almost exclusively on FIRE movement strategies. Halfway through 2021, roughly 50 published videos in, I realized that I could tie my videos ideas together and connect everything I have learned about early retirement to a bigger project: this book. Correction: I didn't realize I *could* do it. I realized I *must* do it.

It started as a spark of an idea but grew into an overwhelming desire. Once the seed was planted, I thought about making this book everyday. I couldn't *not* make it. I had to share this part of my journey and learnings. I wanted to help and inspire others the way I felt inspired. If nothing else, I needed to document this chapter of my life. It was time to get to work. I made a YouTube video announcing that I was writing a book. *"...and it will be out before the end of the year!"*, I declared. That was my way of holding myself accountable.

When I was finished recording that video I remember thinking *"Here we go again!"* I will never forget how excited I was for this book before you to be finished before I put a single word to paper. I quickly outlined 20 chapters to cover in around 150 pages. Clearly brevity is not my strong suit...

How do you write a book that is in your soul—a book that you're passionate about? One day at a time. One chapter at a time. Or in my case, one video twice a week for a year. Thank you for being a part of the coming chapters literally, and this chapter in my life figuratively. I hope this book suits you well to get you on the path and keeps you on the path to financial independence and early retirement.

This book is a snapshot in time so I will not pretend to know it all. I hope that makes it more relatable. I hope you find it easier to follow a guide that's only a few steps, or year ahead of you if you're just getting started. Nobody like a know-it-all anyways... I am an ordinary person who wants to live a an extraordinary life. If you are reading this, I suspect we have a lot in common. Let's do this together.

Writing a book is incredibly challenging but deeply rewarding,

TABLE OF CONTENTS

even if it only makes a difference in one person's life. I hope that person is you.

Don't Miss: Enjoy a companion YouTube video for each chapter linked at the end of this book under "Resources" or find the "Save Half, Retire Fast" playlist. It includes 10 bonus videos! It'll bring each chapter to life and reinforce the core concepts. Subscribe to "The Money Resolution" on YouTube to follow my retire early journey. I will continue to share everything I learn because a rising tide lifts all boats. In the meantime, enjoy this book as your paddle. Let the voyage begin! But first, let me take you back to where it began for me...

Prologue

My FIRE Story

January 1st, 2018. What a miserable unhappy new year. I was sick as a dog to boot. When I woke up that New Year's Day, my financial life was equally unhealthy. It wasn't in total shambles, but it was bad. I had $80,000 in student loan debt and $16,000 in credit card debt and little else to my name. I was making around $55,000 a year, which might sound good and dandy, but I was living in Capitol Hill, a very expensive (see also: fun) part of Seattle. I was splitting a townhouse that I rented for above what I could afford. I was barely getting by and it was getting worse each paycheck.

"How did it get this bad?" I thought. It's simple looking back. It wasn't one thing. It was a series of small, poor decisions that snowballed and put me in this hole. That morning was the turning point—my-come-to-financial-Jesus moment if you will. Laying in bed sick and hungover (poor decision exhibit A), I listened to the pouring rain outside. I started to calculate how much I spent last night and that's when my depression and anger boiled over.

Enough is enough. I've had it!

At that moment I knew I couldn't control my cold, hangover, or how much I spent the night before. But I knew I had to end this spend-more-than-I-earn cycle and fix my financial struggles once and for all. I set a one-word New Year's Resolution: "Money." It's the only resolution I've ever stuck with. Little did I know it would become a lifelong pursuit.

I wrote an entire book about everything I learned and the actions I took that year. I was obsessed. I was a madman finally doing good. I was going to learn all things about money from scratch. I'd be a sponge. It started with a no-spend week. Then I focused on the small things like reducing bills and cutting out the happy hours and any unnecessary spending. I downgraded my car to a small 50cc moped and drove it no matter what, rain or shine. Ubers and $50 tanks of gas were no longer an option.

I earned a promotion and also changed jobs that year, increasing my salary twice. That was critical. You can only reduce your spending so much, but increasing your income is limitless. None of this success happened *to* me or *for* me. I didn't do a few things right and hoped for the best. I made it all happen. I was resolved about it. I had a "no days off" mentality.

I'm skipping ahead for a moment, but the end result was that I got back to net worth zero in less than two years. Two and a half years after that, I'm on track to reach a net worth of $200,000 by the end of 2021.

The most important thing I did in my year of money was I educated myself because school sure didn't teach us this personal finance stuff growing up. I obsessed over finance podcasts and finance YouTube channels. I read a dozen personal finance books—funny enough, reading a dozen books in a year was a failed resolution the prior year.

I first heard about the FIRE movement while reading Vicki Robin's book Your Money Or Your Life. I don't believe the book mentions the FIRE movement by name, but it's widely known as the book that started the FIRE movement. I devoured other books that all reinforced Vicki's core strategies and philosophies such as "Rich Dad, Poor Dad", "The Simple Path to Wealth", "The Automatic Millionaire", "Meet The Frugalwoods", "Financial Freedom", and "The 4-Hour Workweek" for example. Even so, there was something about the FIRE movement itself that was extremely off-putting. As in I *hated* it off-putting.

I remember researching the FIRE movement myself and I quickly found I wasn't the only one turned off by this "movement". As I mentioned, there are a lot of people out there that flat-out hate it. Suze

Orman downright despises it. I'll admit, I found it easy to blindly join this angry mob.

To this day, most of my closest friends are very skeptical about the movement for the same reasons I was. Why do the naysayers hate it and what were my reasons? Let me count the ways and confront these unfounded beliefs:

1. I thought FIRE meant living an extreme, frugal lifestyle where you don't own anything beyond core needs. Think minimalism, but even more extreme. **It's not.** It's being intentional with spending. It's about mindfulness with your money. How you earn it. How you save it. How you invest it. And how you protect it.

2. I thought people were chasing it because they simply hated their job and wanted a way out. Or they were lazy and didn't want to contribute to society in general. **Wrong again**. Many people continue to work in retirement or pursue a passion with full-time efforts. Plus, the word "lazy" is an antonym for how I would describe FIRE individuals. Many of them side hustle and put in dozens of hours a week, beyond a 9 to 5, myself included.

3. I thought FIRE was a cult. This belief was embarrassing so I made a whole video analyzing FIRE and comparing it to cults. Watch if you'd like but spoiler, **it's very much *not* a cult**. There are no official rules or leader or sign-up forms. In fact, lots of people are FIRE without realizing it, as I was. I also discussed this in more detail in Part IV: The Darker Side of FIRE.

4. I thought FIRE seekers only had one hobby: saving as much money as possible at all costs. I assumed all they did day and night was figure out new ways to optimize their finances—how to nickel and dime everything; from comparing rates, to never eating out. Definitely no tipping. Bike to work and of course, live off of rice and beans. **Wrong and wrong**. I don't even feel the need to address this one. That said, there are extreme FIRE seekers and they're the ones that typically make the headlines. Those headlines are likely what turned me off in

the first place.

5. Finally, I hated it because I thought it was out of reach. It sounded like a pipe dream that wasn't realistic for the average person. **I was very wrong about that. I now believe anybody can achieve FIRE**. But again, it's the high-income earners, typically in tech, that save 90% and retire in 3 years that end up making the rounds in the media. However, there are countless average Joe's and Jill's out there, whose story deserves to be heard. They achieved FIRE the boring, simple path way. But nobody is clicking on an article that says "I saved 35% of my income and retired early in 25 years". I'm getting ahead of myself—I discuss more misconceptions on the FIRE movement in Chapter 17.

Throughout 2018 I developed my money mindset, my financial philosophy, and my tactical personal finance strategies with everything I was learning. In a recent 2021 YouTube video about investing, I said I keep it "old school" or I'm an "old soul", which is my way of saying I keep it simple. I make saving and investing automatic. I max out my 401(k), Roth IRA, and HSA 2 years and counting with a low-fee total stock market or S&P 500 index funds from Fidelity, Schwab, or Vanguard.

But the most important decision I made was trying to save half of my post-tax take-home pay in 2019. I got extremely close. I maxed out the 3 aforementioned tax-advantaged accounts. I built up an emergency fund. I saved 90% from my side hustle income. And I made payments towards my still crippling student loan debt (I obliterated my credit card debt in 2018 as my first goal).

But why 50%? Why aim to save half specifically? I was reading Mr. Money Moustache's famous blog post called The Shockingly Simple Math Behind Early Retirement when I discovered this chart:

Savings Rate (Percent)	Working Years Until Retirement
5	66
10	51
15	43
20	37
25	32
30	28
35	25
40	22
45	19
50	17
55	14.5
60	12.5
65	10.5
70	8.5
75	7
80	5.5
85	4
90	Under 3
95	Under 2
100	Zero

I locked onto the center of it. 50…17. It indicated if you achieved a 50% savings rate you can retire in 17 years. My jaw hit the ground. Instantly I thought, "Okay, I'm 33 and in debt but if I commit to this I can retire by age 50." My mantra quickly became: **Save and invest half, retire twice as fast.**

That statement was literal for me at the time. I was going to aim to retire in 17 years instead of 34 (or also likely, never). That chart was all the motivation I needed except for one thing. *I didn't have a why*. Get out of debt? Sure. Quit my job? I didn't hate it and I liked the people. Travel the world? I liked traveling but I'm perfectly happy with one or two trips a year.

I started to identify my *why* halfway through writing my first book The Money Resolution. "Holy crap, people are going to read this and I know in my heart, it will help them", I realized. "Even if it's only friends and family, it will make a difference. It will start conversations at home. People will reach out and ask me questions. And it might even reach and help a stranger or two!"

Then I started my YouTube channel in 2019. It was borderline awful for a year as I bounced around from financial topic to topic with zero camera speaking charisma (that's okay, start messy). But it started to gain some traction in 2020.

I identify my why as freedom, time, and education. It's doing what I want, when I wantfsu, with whom I want to do it with. It's pursuing passions and right now, my passion is helping others get resolved to get good with money via Medium, YouTube, and my self-published books.

That all brings me to today. I've miraculously accelerated my journey these last 4 years—again I'm approaching a $200,000 net worth. My net worth has increased by nearly $300,000 in 4 years. It grew $100,000 in the last year alone. Gradually, the snowball effect, where my debt continued to grow, actually also worked in the opposite direction. I was starting to get rid of this debt and slowly but surely, I increased my net worth. A new, positive snowball was now working in my favor.

A lot has changed in roughly 4 years. Now 36, my current goal is to retire from traditional work by age 45, 9 years from now. 17 years is looking more like 13 after 4 years of working extremely hard to master my money.

To recap:

- I was motivated and resolved about it.
- I gained the knowledge.
- I experienced success which gave me momentum.
- I developed a why which has evolved and will continue to evolve.

- I also discovered a passion that holds myself accountable financially with YouTube.

I still take no days off. I constantly learn new things to share. It helps me remain motivated daily. In fact, being a content creator gets me out of bed most days and I'm extremely grateful for that. I have the FIRE movement core strategies to thank for it all.

In mid-2020 I "joined" the FIRE movement. I was already FIRE by practice, but I was what I now call Denial FIRE. In 2020 I took my FIRE relationship to the next level when I published my first FIRE video. It was my first video that took off organically. In other words, it didn't get views like my other videos only because it was a search-driven topic like credit cards, Costco Hacks, or pet insurance. This video changed everything for me. It's the reason I was able to reach 1,000 subscribers and monetize my YouTube channel in 2020.

I doubled down and tripled down on FIRE content and it helped me grow as a channel, a writer, a creator, and honestly… as a person. I dove in headfirst. I was alive! I once again felt that initial madman obsession with financial literacy, but now it was specific to Financial Independence, Retire Early. I found a dozen FIRE blogs and the Financial Independence subreddit. I read Playing With FIRE and more FIRE books. I subscribed to FIRE-specific YouTube channels. It all fueled my personal fire and creativity.

No days off.

What have I learned about FIRE a few years into my FI journey? And what's ahead?

I learned FIRE is more doable and simple than most people think. It's action-based at first, but then it's mostly auto-pilot once you develop a plan and put it in motion. I also learned anyone can achieve FIRE in any location on any income if they get resolved about it.

At its core, FIRE movement core strategies come down to two simple tactics:

- Live on less than you earn.
- Invest early and often.

There are a dozen different kinds of FIRE types and countless ways to achieve financial independence—building passive income streams or real estate for example—but in its simplest terms, it's about increasing your savings rate and investing that savings wisely and early so you can experience the magic of compound interest. That's when your net worth grows, gradually then suddenly, in the positive direction. It's when your earnings get reinvested and those earnings also earn earnings and it snowballs from there.

And of course, it's critical you develop a strong why of FI as I've talked about. It's not about running from something, it's about running to something. It's about having the *option* to retire early. It's choice. It's freedom. It's becoming a master of your time—which is the most valuable non-renewable resource we all have. And you need a strong moral financial compass to get there.

Financial stability also gave me confidence that debt sucked away from me and maybe this is too much information but it's true: it helped me combat the anxiety monster and even panic attacks caused mostly by the financial struggles that I battled internally every day. But going through that is a perspective I take with me and take seriously now. I know first-hand how much debt affects your mental health.

I've alluded to it by now, but another thing I discovered, or rather re-discovered, that I didn't expect in this journey was my creativity. I used to distract myself in my free time with sports and video games and movies and bars and concerts and dating and friends and I could go on. But by cutting out a lot of those distractions, I freed up a lot of time (it helps that I found the perfect life partner too, of course!). I used that time to be creative and take risks with that pent-up creativity I knew I had inside of me. It now pours out of me.

I write and make videos and I finally understand what it means when people say "If you find work you love, you'll never work another day of your life", and this isn't even my full-time gig.

I want to leverage this newly found creativity to help other people avoid the financial mistakes I made. I hope to encourage people to have difficult conversations about personal finance and talk openly about money with their friends and loved ones. But I don't want to push FIRE on anybody. The FIRE movement is not for everyone, but it can be for anyone. It's worth exploring because we can all learn from it. I want to encourage people to increase their savings rate and pursue financial independence, whether they desire early retirement or not.

"Not everyone should pursue an early retirement, but everyone should pursue financial independence." -Ty Roberts

You can improve your life by pursuing FI. Having an emergency fund and financial security opens up doors and reduces so much stress. You might find, as I have, financial freedom even makes it easier to give back, help others, and make a difference—especially if you don't get fulfillment with your daily 9 to 5 grind.

In terms of what's ahead in this book, it's all about getting on the path to financial independence and how to stay on the path, ideally automatically. Yes, it has all the numbers and tactics but it's also about mindset. It's about finding your why, what you're running to. It's honest, open, and transparent. It's my story because if I can do it, I believe anyone can. It's about wanting more out of your life and the strategies to achieve whatever it is you want. It's the rules of the game and the reward you earn for achieving financial victory.

"Save Half, Retire Fast" is a positive, encouraging book—free of fear tactics. It's good ol' fashion financial advice, so you can achieve success one day at a time. And ultimately, it's about enjoying the journey along the way because that actually is the best part. If you're not living your life on your quest for FI, you're doing it wrong.

I view this book as part 3 in a series. The Money Resolution was how to get out of debt and climb back to net worth zero—my story and the financial basics. Money, You Can Hack It was how to go from net worth zero to $100,000, a six-figure net worth—where creativity and fun meet personal finance.

Save Half, Retire Fast is how to grow from six figures to ideally seven. From $100,000 (or wherever you're starting) to $1,000,000—a nice round number that many people aim for to retire. It's all things

FIRE movement and my journey so far on my way to 1 million, ideally by age 45.

And even though "fast" is in the title, that's not a promise or guarantee. But when it comes to FIRE strategies and consistency, it so happens if you do enough things right, fast financial independence happens as a result. What you decide to do when you reach financial independence is ultimately up to you. That sounds an awful lot like freedom.

Gradually, then suddenly… free.

Introduction

Why You Should Pursue Financial Independence

Why?

It's fitting we start this financial independence journey with this question. I will ask you to pause and reflect often on your why in the chapters that follow. That's because if you're pursuing financial independence for the wrong reasons, you'll be more likely to give in or give up when the going gets tough. And you won't fully enjoy and appreciate the journey along the way.

Why financial independence? Why now? It's difficult to achieve after all. Pursuing financial independence takes a lot of time, energy, and sacrifices that will test your resolve throughout.

That said, there are more people pursuing financial independence now than ever. FIRE movement popularity has accelerated over the last decade. Why has it become so popular? There has never been a better time to chase financial independence than now, and there have never been more reasons to achieve it. In a future chapter, I'll also explain how it's actually *easier* than ever to achieve as well. No, not easy. But easier than a decade or two decades prior.

Why did I finally decide to take on early retirement as a goal? The reality is, I realized mindlessly trading my time for money via the traditional 9 to 5 grind for nearly 50 years until I hopefully retire on time is risky. Let's start there as I share my reasons for why I pursue financial independence and early retirement and why you might want to reject the status quo as well:

Job security is an illusion

In my fifteen years in the workforce, I've had several experiences with organizations that had to downsize. I've seen entire teams and departments get eliminated in an instant. Right out of college, I joined Teach for America and I was laid off after one year of teaching. I was desperate to find another job, and remained jobless until I was luckily rehired 3 days before the next school year started. That experience has greatly impacted my life and reconstructed my mindset about job security.

If you work for a company, you're likely to have far less job security than you are aware of. It's a harsh reality people don't consider until it happens to them. Businesses fail, need to downsize, get purchased, or the new leadership makes drastic changes. If you solely rely your livelihood on that one job, you're a step away from unemployment. If you're living paycheck to paycheck, this thought can be downright terrifying.

No amount of education or experience can eliminate the possibility of being let go at a moment's notice, leaving you to scramble. You might even accept the first job offered to you, even if it's one you're not passionate about.

To be financially independent, you release the baggage or worry about your job performance or a company remaining successful to receive a monthly income. Taken further, diversifying your income via investing, side hustles, and even passive income projects will aid you in your journey as we'll discuss. This mindset, understanding, and quest for financial independence even led me to entrepreneurship in terms of being a content creator and an author. You might be surprised where it leads you!

You can exit the rat race

The rat race is a system that was created for the working class to stay in a constant loop of working 9-5 jobs Monday through Friday chasing the next paycheck or raise. Once you reach financial independence, you are no longer participating in that race.

Oftentimes, traditional work won't allow you to retire until you're 67 in the US. In today's society, you work 40 to 50 years only to "enjoy" retirement for 15 years. This doesn't sound like a fair deal to me, especially if you're at a job that you don't enjoy. Add government intervention, dried up social security benefits, tax increases, and likely changes to the retirement age and you are on track to work even longer.

On the other hand, financial independence allows you to pursue opportunities that might have otherwise seemed high-risk or unattainable. In the beginning, there will be challenges. However, with determination and resilience, you have the power to reach greater heights and turn your dreams into a reality, whatever they may be. And you can do so while you're younger and healthier.

Financial independence puts you in a better position to help others

In life, you should absolutely aim to help yourself as a top priority. Then, when possible, you should aim to help others. Pay it forward for all of the people and resources that helped you. This has become extremely important to me in terms of my why of FI. I genuinely get excited to learn and share what I'm learning—to share the things that are helping me and moving the needle financially and otherwise.

If we want to live an extraordinary life, we need to serve and impact other people's lives in a positive way. If you can find a way to provide solutions to a select group of people's common problems, you'll feel fulfilled. Time gives you more opportunities to do so. When I was living paycheck to paycheck and deep in debt, I found it hard to find opportunities to give back to my community or help others. I also found it hard to learn new skills or even try new hobbies. Speaking of...

You can enjoy the gift of time and live life to the fullest

Don't we all desire this? Once reaching financial independence, you will have more time to spend time with family and friends, and do activities that make you happy. Seeking financial independence won't guarantee you become a millionaire, but it will buy something far more priceless: *time*. Not only would you have extra time in your day, but likely enough money to supplement experiences that you've dreamt about doing. You can travel the world and see amazing sights you've only seen in movies. I personally want to attend sporting events across the country and try new hobbies without worrying about the cost of entry.

Time is of the essence, and we're only getting older each day. The goal is to reach financial freedom, so you maximize your time of basking in the beauty of life, rather than retiring with your 401(k) when you're grey and old at age 67 or beyond.

If family and having kids is a priority for you, being financially free allows you to have more time to spend raising kids and being involved in their lives. You have the ability to work or not, and have better time management within your day. Achieving financial independence means having control back in your life so you can direct your time and attention to those you care about most.

Your why of FI

Hating your job or looking for a quick fix to happiness are not reasons to chase financial independence. It's about running *to* something, not *from* something. If you're unsure about your why, think about what you would do if all your current expenses were covered. I'm not talking about having extra income and spending more. **What would you do with your time?** That's a great exercise to work through and reflect on.

I challenge you to come up with a written why today. Turn it into a mission statement. Keep that mission statement in sight, and in mind. When you're first getting started with your why, a few key bullets will do. I shared my first attempt at the beginning of my second book. It was only a few words: freedom, time, and education. Next, it's important to know why it can and likely will change over time. That's why it's critical you revisit it every year or so. It will likely evolve and expand as you live and learn.

Time is your most precious non-renewable resource. FI (financial independence) allows you to earn more time back. Time is on your side when you get on the path and stay on the path to financial independence. In a sense, my why of FI is to become the master of my time. It's to be able to spend every single day doing what I want, when I want, with the people that matter most to me. FI doesn't solve all of your problems, but it makes life much easier than if you're living paycheck to paycheck, unsure about job security, and underwater in debt. FI isn't the only path to long-term happiness and more time, and it isn't the single answer to happy life, but it is the path I believe in and one I'll continue to pursue. Since I discovered the FIRE movement I can honestly say I've never been happier or more successful personally and financially. It has given me a north star—one I hope can guide you as well.

The final key piece of my why is to live a life without regrets. I never want to look back and regret wasting the best years of my life mentally and physically doing something I wasn't passionate about or feeling trapped. I'd rather live free. And in the meantime live *inspired.*

Never forget: When your why is clear, your how becomes easy. If it's not clear now it will be by the end of the book.

Save and invest half, retire twice as fast. Get your time and freedom back. Thank you for allowing me to be your guide on the how. Let's begin.

Part I

First Things First

CHAPTER ONE

Save and Invest Half, Retire Twice as Fast

50% is difficult, but here's why it matters

Over a recent 5 year span, the US personal savings rate ranged from 6.3% to 8.8%. That was until 2020 when the pandemic hit. According to statista.com, in April of 2020, the personal savings rate hit a whopping 33.7%. While the reason for this spike was caused by the pandemic, I am optimistic many will continue to save more money in a post-Covid world.

When it comes to building your wealth, your savings rate is a crucial factor. If you can save half of your income (a 50% savings rate), you can reach financial independence in as little as 17 years, on *any* income.

What is financial independence? It's when the money you have saved and invested for retirement earns enough that you can live off of it for the rest of your life. That means:

- Work is optional.
- You're free to pursue your passions.
- You can tackle your bucket list.
- You can spend more time with your loved ones.
- You can give time and or money to help people

And so much more…

Saving half sounds a bit extreme on the surface, right? It's likely far different than what you've heard. Conventional wisdom says to save 10% or 20% if you're an overachiever. Perhaps you've heard of the 50/30/20 rule. That suggests you should spend 50% of your money on needs, 30% on wants, and put 20% away into savings. I'm here to say… that's good, but not enough.

Let's say you made $100,000 and saved 20%. You'd have $20,000 to your name after a year. Not bad. However, if you made $40,000 (the Median US salary in 2019) and saved half, you'd have the same amount saved as someone making 150% more than you. **It's not how much you make, it's how much you save and invest that matters most.** The sooner you start saving, the more time your money can grow and compound exponentially. That's the power of compound interest. This is when the interest your money makes gets reinvested and gains even more interest and the cycle snowballs from there.

The reality is, 20% is *far* better than the average person saves, so I support a 20% savings rate as a starting point. But let's talk about the power of going from saving 20% to 25% to 40% to HALF of your income:

If you make $50,000 and save 20%, but you get started at age 35 with nothing saved, will you be able to retire at age 67? Nope. According to the retirement calculator at NerdWallet, you'll be about $300,000 off.

What if you saved 30% of your pre-tax income, even as a late starter at age 40. That gets you 82% of the way there. How about a 40% savings rate at age 40 starting from $0? You can retire 2 years early at 65. How about a 50% savings rate at age 40, assuming you'll continue to spend the same amount in retirement? You're retiring at age 59, with an incredibly late start.

If you're starting from zero invested at age 50, I highly recommend you aim for a 50% savings rate as a starting point. If you do so, you can absolutely retire on time at age 67. I hope that is refreshing to hear.

Here's the thing to remember no matter where you are on your financial planning journey: **Time is your biggest asset. Taking control of your financial future is life-changing.** Your attitude and hard work are within your control.

"Whether you think you can or you think you can't, you're right." -Henry Ford

What factors are out of your control?

- When you get a raise or promotion.
- Your job security.
- Your work hours if you're part-time.
- Mistakes you've made in the past that put you in debt.
- What the person on the other side of the interview table thinks about hiring you for that new, better-paying job you want so badly.
- A black swan event like a pandemic, a war, or some other unforeseen circumstance like a stock market crash.

Before we dive head-first into your first how-to tips, it's important I take a moment to explain what my definition of saving is. You can save money in one of two main ways: setting aside money for retirement or making a payment towards the principle of debts. Saving is anything you do with your money that positively increases your net worth.

In terms of saving for the long-term, that includes:

- Money put into an emergency fund
- Investing within a 401(k), IRA, or other tax-benefits retirement account
- Contributing to a 529 Plan or otherwise saving for a child's education
- Money you put in an online high-interest savings account
- Change in your piggy bank. That's an account, right?

Examples of debt payments that count as saving include:

- Principle paid on higher-interest debts such as your credit cards
- Principle paid on lower-interest debts such as your mortgage

Payment that goes to interest is not paying off debt and does not count as saving money because it is not impacting the principal balance. Let's say you accrue $500 a month in credit card debt and decide to pay the minimum. Let's assume that minimum is $50 and that payment only covers $50 owed in interest. You are not saving any money. In fact, your debt will infinitely increase in this awful scenario. This is what they want. This is how credit card companies win. If you were to make a $100 payment instead, you are saving $50 which is the amount that would go towards your principle balance.

If you are keeping your money for the long-term or reducing debt, you're saving it. The goal is the same: spend less and increase your net worth.

What does *not* count as saving? Pooling money together for a short-term spending goal. For example, let's say I want the next latest and greatest iPhone when it comes out. I might decide to save $100 a month towards the phone purchase so that I can pay for it in cash in full. This is smart because I will not take on debt over it. However, I am still technically spending money in this scenario. I am not investing $100 monthly. I am not paying down the principle on my student loans. I am thinking ahead and avoiding debt, but the phone won't grow in value. I won't use it in retirement. This does not count as saving.

The same is true for a new or used car, Christmas presents for the family, a vacation, and concert tickets. You should absolutely budget and save for those purchases, but that is not the savings we're talking about when I say "save half." In those scenarios, you are saving money to spend money. This does not increase your net worth or count towards your savings rate. Some people view saving to spend as saving money. It's this kind of thinking that allows people to falsely believe that they are good money savers. These are the people that wonder why they have nothing to show for their hard work at the end of the year, each and every year.

Save half. Spend half. Retire early. Get your life and freedom back. *Great, makes sense and sounds awesome, but how do you actually do it?* Let's get straight to your first tips, your first steps on your financial freedom journey…

CHAPTER TWO

How To Save Half of Your Income

Half is more than possible with these strategies

What's the secret to saving half of your income so you can achieve financial independence? Reduce your expenses and increase your income. I know that sounds easier said than done. You need to know where you can find the biggest reductions in spending as well as what to do with those savings when you earn them. Don't simply bank the savings and extra income. Invest the savings—all of your money beyond your monthly expenses and emergency fund. Park the money where it will turn into more money. This is how you achieve financial independence far faster than most. If you can reduce your spending and invest this money that you have saved wisely, you can retire a decade or two earlier than you thought was possible.

Here are your first actionable tips to get you on the path and keep you on the path to financial independence. We'll explore many of these topics further in future chapters.

Understand your why, your numbers, and set goals

As with most things, getting started is half the battle. Take some time to lay the groundwork and create a roadmap for yourself, so that you know where you are going and how to get there. Here are your actionable tips in bullet-format.

- Determine your "why" I discussed in the Introduction. Why do you want to save half your income? What are your goals for retirement?
- Find your current savings rate. What can you do to increase that rate over the next year? A 1% increase a month can have a huge impact! We'll cover exactly how to calculate your savings in a future chapter.
- Spend time with the retirement calculators from NerdWallet and Bankrate to make sure your savings rate aligns with your goals.

Develop your financial awareness. Know what you spend and where you're starting from.

For some people, cash is a weakness—if they have it, they will most definitely spend it and have no idea where it went. For others, credit cards are basically imaginary money—they swipe or tap and pay no attention to the total amount. You probably already know which camp you are in, so now it's time to drill down and pay attention to where exactly that money goes.

- Track every dollar for a month. Keep your receipts and use a spreadsheet, utilize an app, whatever works best for you—but track *every* dollar.
- Analyze your monthly spending and see exactly how much you can save with this newfound financial awareness.
- Finesse your numbers and goals from there. Prior planning prevents poor performance.

Reduce your 3 biggest expenses

Why only the top 3? Because of the 80/20 rule. Focus on the 20% of your efforts that will get you 80% of the results. When reducing your biggest expenses, you'll get that dopamine hit and find the motivation to start making cuts in other areas. Use that momentum!

- Housing: If you can reduce your housing from 38% of your income to 28% of your income, you could give yourself a 10% raise! If you reduce it to 18%, that's a 20% raise. Get a roommate. Rent out a spare room on Airbnb. There's always a way. You simply need a little creativity and willingness to take action to find it.
- Food: Delete the food ordering apps. Cook instead. Consider ordering your groceries online so you're not tempted to buy those cookies and fancy cheese when you're in the store.
- Transportation: Live closer to work or take public transportation. Consider your opportunity cost. What else could you be doing with your time instead of commuting?

Become a financial minimalist and live frugally

This isn't going to happen overnight. It might sound cliche but small tweaks and consistency yield the greatest results—it also prevents you from burning out and giving up.

- When shopping, create a list and stick with it. If you are considering a big purchase, wait a week. If you still think you really need, or desperately want, this thing after a week of thinking over the cost, go for it. But you may find that you really don't need it or, better yet, you forget about it completely.
- Save (and invest!) the money you almost blew. If you cook your food instead of getting takeout, bank that $15 as if you spent it.
- Stay in and use current streaming platform subscriptions to watch movies. If you go to the movies, you're more likely to pay for the ticket, popcorn, drinks, and gas money. All this extra money can be saved!

Get comfortable living uncomfortably and pay yourself first.

This may seem counterintuitive, but Warren Buffett advises it and he didn't get to be the world's 4th wealthiest person by mistake. If you're going to live comfortably in retirement, you have to prioritize paying yourself first now. Here's how:

- Automate your savings. Don't let the money hit your checking account because you can't spend what you don't see or have.
- Prioritize your tax-advantaged retirement accounts first. If you do this, you're saving consistently *and* investing using the dollar-cost averaging method, which we'll discuss more in future chapters.
- If you are married or live with a partner, try the "Starve and Stack" method: use one salary to live off of (ideally the smaller one) and completely save the other.

Ask for a raise or earn more money with side hustles and save 100% of new money

What if you've cut as many expenses as you reasonably can and you still aren't hitting your savings goal? One way to stay on track with your goals is by increasing your income. You can only reduce your spending so much, but you income earning potential is limitless.

- The easiest way to increase your income is to ask for a raise. Take some time to research and reflect on the value you bring, then have an open and honest conversation with your boss. If you do get that raise, promotion, or bonus, put it all into savings and investments.
- Pick up a side hustle. Do you have a special skill or talent that others will pay money to learn or otherwise benefit from? There is a side hustle out there for literally anyone. Find the one that calls to you and save all of the earnings.
- Start a business online. Keep your team and expenses very small. Become a company of one. Find a specific problem you can solve for a specific audience. Be consistent, patient, and constantly learn. You can go out of your comfort zone and

maybe even do what I did, by starting a YouTube channel or creating a course.

Note about income: The more money you make, the more prone you become to spending it. The best way to avoid an inflated lifestyle is by automatically saving it. Celebrating a raise or promotion with dinner and drinks or treating yourself to a new power suit can really add up and eat away at your financial goals. Celebrate your wins, but stay the course and commit to your savings goal. There will be plenty to celebrate later when you're financially independent! If you make more, save more. If you can learn to live on $25,000 and continue living on $25,000 when you make $100,000, that's when incredible savings magic happens and accelerates your journey exponentially!

Surround yourself with like-minded individuals

This one is simple but incredibly important.

- Surround yourself with friends and family that support your goals and lifestyle.
- Have open and honest conversations with your partner, closest friends, and family about money and financial goals.
- Join Facebook or LinkedIn groups to continue to expand your finance-minded network.

You're the average of the 5 people you spend the most time with, so choose wisely!

Don't look at your paycheck as money for bills and hope you have something leftover. You deserve the money you worked so hard for. Look at your paycheck as yours to save and invest. Take it step by step and day by day. Do a little something today, make another great decision tomorrow. Flex your frugality muscles daily and they'll get noticeably stronger each day and month.

Actionable finance tips are great, but let's discuss something I love even more: *money hacks*. Specifically an incredible mental money hack I personally employ to stay on track for early retirement.

CHAPTER THREE

The #1 Reason People Don't Retire Early

Money is 90% mental. You get to decide what's possible.

At the beginning of my journey, I connected dots when it comes to retirement and a possible reason why early retirement feels so elusive for many. It's a mental hurdle or block that's easy to jump over or break through when you identify it and internalize it.

Parkinson's Law

The reason people don't retire early, or even on time, is because of a concept known as Parkinson's Law. What is Parkinson's Law? It's the idea that work expands so as to fill the time available for its completion.

Why don't we retire before the traditional retirement age of 67 in the US? It's because we set age 67 as a mental deadline and we expand work (quite literally, when you think about it) to take up that amount of time. This is exactly why I say, don't be afraid to aim high when it comes to when you want to retire. If you tell yourself you're going to retire at 67, odds are you're going to retire at 67. Alternatively, if you decide, right now today, you're going to retire at 55 or even 50, odds are you're going to make it happen as long as you decide that's your deadline.

It only takes a minute

In a way, Parkinson's Law rings true on many levels when it comes to people and how long it takes us to complete tasks or projects, no matter how big or small. The simplest way nearly all of us do this daily is how much time it takes to get ready in the morning. Personally, if I have 30 minutes, I'll take 30 minutes. If I somehow miss my alarm and have 5 minutes to get out of the door, I'm out of the door in 5 minutes, miraculously.

Let's say you have a big work project with an end-of-week deadline. Oftentimes, we wait until the final day or final hours to tackle it. Does this sound like you, too? It's funny how if you wait until the last minute, it only takes a minute to do it. Some of us are even proud of how well we work under pressure. I know I personally think I do my best work under pressure. But, what if we instead found a way to put that pressure on ourselves on Tuesday instead of Friday at 3 pm?

Set new deadlines

When I sat down to outline and write this chapter, I gave myself 1 hour. A typical chapter takes me 5 hours or more to produce from idea to final edits. However, I'm determined to finish my personal 1-hour deadline to reinforce this point to myself.

As I mentioned, I run a YouTube channel and I typically spend 12–15 hours on each video. However, I once had 2 hours to make a whole video from scratch because I was taking my computer in to get repaired. The repair was going to take 10 days, but I had an upload goal. Sure enough, I figured out a way to get it done. I decided to film it in one take. Was it my best video? Not by any means. But I've learned, oftentimes done is better than perfect.

In that situation, I had an appointment, so I had a hard and fixed deadline to motivate myself. But sometimes you may have to trick yourself a bit. As an example, if you're like me and you inevitably always arrive 10 minutes late, set all your clocks ahead by 10 minutes. When it comes to retirement and you are content with retiring at age 67, prepare as if you might miss that deadline and aim for age 60 instead. That way, if it takes you extra time or the market isn't cooperating in a downturn, you'll get there by 67 no doubt.

Diamonds are created under pressure. So try this mental hack and create something beautiful.

Forcing the issue

Don't get me wrong. You can't force the issue if it's unrealistic for the task or assignment at hand. When it comes to retirement, the same is true. If you're 60 or older right now and you have $1,000 saved for retirement, the reality is the reality. But, if you're 25, 30, 40, or even 45 now, you can absolutely retire early if you get resolved about it and set a new closer goalpost in your mind.

Let me remind you of my personal mantra again: *"Save and invest half, retire twice as fast."*

Using shockingly simple math from the Mr. Money Moustache blog, you can retire in as little as 17 years if you save half. Possibly sooner, depending on where you're starting from and how the markets do over that span—especially if you sprinkle in a side hustle or a passive income stream. If you're 40 years old, you can absolutely set a goal to retire at age 57 or even 55 as a stretch goal if you can save and invest half as a starting point. If you're 30 now and you save 30% of your pre-tax income, you can retire by 58, nearly a whole decade sooner than most in the US.

Set yourself a deadline, get educated, and get resolved about it. Surround yourself with like-minded people, keep your goal in sight and in mind, and share your goal with family and friends.

Start today

I challenge you to reflect on Parkinson's Law yourself, the idea that tasks or goals take as long as the amount of time we give ourselves to complete them.

In what areas of your life does this hold true? How can you take this idea and help yourself be more productive or more successful? Or even have more fun?

You can drag your feet researching the perfect family vacation plan *or* you can tell yourself: *this weekend I'm going to book the flights, the hotel, and find 3 great family activities while we're there.* You could even create a reward or punishment system to hold yourself accountable. *I earn ice cream when I finish X. I'll sleep in on Saturday morning if I complete Y by Friday night. No TV until I tackle Z.*

When I was new to a city in California, I decided I wanted to join a men's softball team. After weeks of dragging my feet on the idea, I went on a message board and found a team that needed a free agent that day. Finally, I was out there playing ASAP instead of researching for weeks or months. I thought about starting a YouTube channel for a year. One day, I filmed a terrible video on my phone and hit publish without overthinking it. That turned out to be one of my best decisions to date.

You can start that side hustle next month. You can get that business idea off the ground next year when you get some funding or you can try to earn side hustle money by the end of today to prove to yourself you can. Aim to earn $100 this weekend. You can test out that business idea online by the end of the month to see if there actually is a market for it. Make a survey about it *now*. Get started *today*.

Set your goals

I've shared my goals publicly as a way to hold myself accountable. I'm aiming to "retire" from traditional work by age 45. I'm 35 now. I was worth -$80,000 as a ballpark at age 32. I've increased my net worth by more than $250,000 in 3 years and 6 months. How? I got resolved about it. If you want to know the specifics, I documented it all in my first book The Money Resolution. In 2020 I set a big goal. It was to create my first finance course. Guess when that course launched? December. It took me all year because I gave myself until the end of the year.

Alternatively, I wrote and self-published my first book with zero self-publishing knowledge in less than 2 months. My second book took me 15 months because I didn't set a deadline. It took me two days to record and edit the audiobook though because I was determined to finish it in a weekend. I wouldn't accept not finishing it in 48 hours and I checked off a huge to-do box and created a passive income stream in the process. This book? It launched on December 31, 2021, because I set a goal to finish it by the end of the year. Yes, I cut it close. But it would have been another 6 months or a year of work if I didn't have that self-imposed deadline. It also may have been worse quality with unfocused attention over that timespan.

Accomplish anything

Admittedly, people get turned off by the FIRE movement because they think all people seeking FIRE are aiming to retire in their mid-30s. Some do, but many retire in their 40s or even late 50s. Any years of your working life you can get back is a blessing and well worth the effort. That's what FIRE is about.

They say you can do anything when you put your mind to it. I mostly agree, but I'll be more specific: You can accomplish anything when you attach a strict deadline to it and get resolved about it. Gain 10 years of freedom and time back by applying this concept to your retirement. Induce demand or desire and reduce the time to get there. Move the goalpost closer in your mind and you'll do great work under this new self-imposed "pressure" so to speak. Set new deadlines and make beautiful diamonds.

It starts with deciding. It continues with daily action…

CHAPTER FOUR

The 1% Rule of Money

"Constant repetition carries conviction." -Robert Collier

If you're familiar with the financial 1% rule of money, mine is far different. Mine has nothing to do with buying and renting real estate. The 1% rule of money is a challenge. It's to dedicate 1% of your day to working on your financial life. That's 14 minutes and 24 seconds a day. I challenge you to do that for 30 straight days.

"Working on your financial life" is vague on purpose. You will create and choose your own adventure. You can learn about money, make one good financial decision, track your money, or update your budget if you keep one. You can also reflect on your spending, savings, and financial goals—getting your money mentality right so you can develop a growth mindset.

If 14 minutes and 24 seconds working on your money daily sounds like a lot, consider that most doctors, scientists, and the internet agree that 30 minutes of exercise daily is extremely good for you.

I'm not a doctor or scientist, but as a personal finance nerd, I can assure you, working on your financial health for 14 minutes and 24 seconds a day is extremely good for you. That's only 1 hour and 41 minutes a week—the length of a standard movie. That's 7 hours and 7 minutes a month. The Lord of The Rings movie trilogy is 2 hours longer than that!

I recently learned that people that participate in fantasy football spend close to 8 hours a *week* on their team on average. Even if this isn't you, this example shows most of us can find 1 hour and 41 minutes a week to put towards our finances!

If you spent 2% of your day working on your physical health and 1% of your day working on your financial health, you would drastically improve your life. That's 30 minutes of exercise and 15 minutes improving your financial life daily. That's the ultimate resolution. I'm not big on specific concrete resolutions. Instead, I prefer to focus on changing habits and lifestyles. That's where my book The Money Resolution started. Here's the first line from my first book:

"Money. That was my New Year's resolution one year ago. And as vague as that is, it was the only one I've ever stuck with."

Challenge yourself to take on the 1% rule of money 30 Day Challenge: spend at least 14 minutes and 24 seconds a day working on your personal finances. Here's a sample week of what this could look like to show you that not only is this 30-day challenge important, it can be fun and very doable.

Sunday

Sundays are a great day to think about the week ahead and spend some time planning. Perhaps it's creating a meal plan or tackling meal prep for lunch for the week to save on food. It could be paying bills like student loans, credit card balances, or car payments. Start the week right financially with your 1% rule by holding yourself accountable and taking financial action for 14 minutes and 24 seconds of your day.

Monday

On Monday, head to the library and snag a personal finance book or two for free. That might take you 15 minutes or more, so technically you don't even have to crack the book open yet. Plan to spend about an hour with this book during your challenge. If you have a way to read digitally (the Kindle app on any phone or tablet works) try that.

Many libraries allow digital downloads so you can get reading right away. Or keep reading this one of course!

Tuesday

Check out a personal finance podcast while doing the dishes, walking the dog, or [insert chore here]. I recommend The Stacking Benjamins Show, How To Money, and Choose FI. Pop on the latest episode or scan through episodes until you find a topic you find interesting. The styles of these shows are all quite different, so try an episode of each so you can find the style of finance podcast you enjoy the most.

Wednesday

Find out your credit score for free in minutes. There are 3 major credit bureaus: Transunion, Experian, and Equifax. You can get 1 free credit report from each once a year via the site AnnualCreditReport.com. You can request all 3 at once, but I actually recommend you stagger them every 3 or 4 months throughout the year. The benefit of getting all 3 at once is you can compare them side by side. The benefit of staggering them is you can keep an eye on your credit score throughout the year.

Thursday

Do the easiest and most fun thing of all: wrap change from your piggy bank and take it to the bank. Yup, like when you were a kid. If you have change or bills lying around, put it in savings. It's a mindless activity and gets you outside. Don't take it to a Coinstar machine and turn it in for a gift card. Take it to the bank and put it in your savings, so you aren't tempted to spend it mindlessly.

Friday

I wrote this on a Friday and it should take you 7 minutes or so to read this chapter. If you're reading this on a Friday, read one more chapter until the end and you're done for the day. I also have a YouTube channel with weekly videos. I made 100 videos in 2021, many of which are companion videos for chapters in this very book at the end! Find a list of those videos in the end under Resources. It's worth noting, most of my videos are around 14:24 in length. Coincidence? Now you know it's a subtle nod to my 1% rule of money.

Saturday

Take 15 minutes to snag my free One-Page Challenge Sheet and organize it. It's interactive so you can input your challenge and results without printing it if you'd like. Take the time to create a calendar by hand and fill out the 30 boxes. Day 1: You can write "Read 2 chapters from #SaveHalfBook". Day 2: You can write "Create 1% rule of money challenge plan". If you do, take about 15 minutes to organize all of your thoughts and roadmap. I highly recommend you plot out your actions ahead of time to make it a no-brainer to keep up. If nothing else, my one-pager has tons of ideas to get you thinking.

FINAL THOUGHTS AND TAKEAWAYS

Your 1%, your daily 14:24, can be anything related to improving your financial life. It might be learning. It could be organizing your finances. It might be creating a debt payoff plan or making a payment. You can reduce or eliminate a bill. It might be my favorite: making money! Researching and buying your first stock or index fund. Return something you recently bought you don't have a need for. Take a finance course!

Get your free guide at www.TheMoneyResolution.com, fill out your 30-day sheet, and get started. I made this guide because it's the exact kind of thing I wish existed when I started my Money Resolution in 2018, the year I changed my financial life for good. Get excited about trying and facing your fears. Get excited about getting organized and finally having a plan, or in this case a challenge—and who doesn't love a good 30-day challenge? I can assure you,

(financial) "Success is the sum of small efforts repeated day in and day out"
-Robert Collier

When you do start to discover wins and find momentum, 1+1 can equal 3. It's exactly like compound interest. Gradually, then suddenly, you will be successful. But ultimate success begins with goals, and setting your financial independence goal requires key numbers and some easy math. When you're ready, let's work through your numbers next!

CHAPTER FIVE

How to Calculate Your FIRE Number

The exact formula to calculate how much you need to retire

As I've covered previously, once you reach your FI number, work becomes optional. What you do after reaching FI is totally up to you. Retire. Don't retire. Work part-time. Pursue a hobby. That's the point of financial independence: Freedom. Options. Flexibility.

What is a FI number?

It's the amount of money you need to have invested so that you can live off of earned dividends, interest, and capital gains from your investments, conceivably forever. Done right, you'll leave the principle intact long-term, and it will continue to earn you money. With the right strategy, the 4% rule (which we'll cover), you can live off of your retirement portfolio and investments indefinitely. In other words, you no longer need to trade your time for money because you won't ever run out of money with a reasonable degree of certainty.

Why does this financial number matter?

Your FI number is essentially your finish line. I also like to call it the *starting line to fully living*. It's your ultimate long-term big goal. As you see your hard work pay off and see yourself getting closer to that big goal number, you'll become more motivated.

Saving and investing more is good and great. But how much? That's where the financial independence number calculation comes in. Don't worry; it's not complicated. My goal is for you to be able to calculate your FI number confidently and accurately.

Your FI number may feel overwhelming when you calculate it. The length of time to get there might seem incredibly long or even unrealistic. This is why many don't get started or develop an *I'll deal with it later* mentality OR *I'm not going to save money so I can spend it later in life. I'd rather spend it now and enjoy life.* That's fine… if you want to work until your final days.

That mindset is reserved for people that think happiness comes from spending money on things or doing *stuff*. It's for people that think saving more money means you can't buy anything, do anything, or travel anywhere. That's not true if you have a plan.

Even if retiring early isn't your end goal, once you know your number, you can find your annual savings rate needed to retire on time. It's easy to lose sight of your goal and end destination if you don't have one. If you do that, it's easy to fall back into bad habits and stop tracking your progress.

Step 1: Determine your annual expenses.

In other words, how much money do you need every year to live on average? This part can actually be a bit of a process to figure out unless you're someone who already budgets and tracks your spending consistently. The simplified way you can do this is to look back at your last 30 days of spending. Once you have that number, multiply it by 12 to determine your annual expenses. This is a great starting point if you want to work through these steps quickly to get a general idea of your FI number. So, $4,000 a month on all needs and wants is $48,000 a year. Keep in mind, 30 days is a small sample size, and your spending fluctuates during different times of the year (think vacation, big purchases, holidays, etc).

I recommend reviewing 6 months of spending and averaging that. A great way to do that is by using online software. Step 1 is simple, but does take time. Determine your annual expenses by tracking every dollar spent in the last month or taking an average of the last few months of spending, and multiply by 12.

Step 2: Multiply your annual expenses by 25.

This is incredibly simple compared to step 1. Let's say someone calculated their projected annual expenses in retirement, and that was $40,000. They would then multiply that number by 25 to find their FI number of $1 million.

If you're curious:

- $50,000 in annual expenses comes out to $1.25M
- $75,000 in annual expenses comes out to $1.875M.
- $100,000 in annual expenses comes out to $2.5M.

If you're married, combine your annual expenses and multiply by 25. That is your FIRE number as a couple. By why 25x? It is not because we are assuming 25 years in retirement. It's because of the 4% rule.

The 4% Rule

This is, in short, your safe annual withdrawal rate once you reach financial independence. Once you have a portfolio built up to your FI number, the 4% rule helps you understand how much you can withdraw from your investment portfolio annually to live off of such that you won't run out of money in retirement. If you withdraw 4%, what happens to the other 96%? It remains invested. What happens to invested money? It grows. This annual rate of growth hovers around 7–8% on average historically.

Of course, growth is volatile. Some years it's negative, even double-digit negative during a recession which lasts 13 months on average. Some years your portfolio value will increase by the same amount. Overall though, in the long run, it'll be up. The 4% rule comes from the Trinity Study in 1998 from Trinity College in Texas. In short, they analyzed different types of portfolios and real historical investment data to determine how long portfolios would last at different withdrawal rates. It showed in almost all scenarios, a 4% withdrawal rate was the "sweet spot" for not running out of money in retirement.

Even during the Great Depression and the market crash in the early 70s, money never ran out before 33 years. The study even accounts for inflation. In other words, if you took out $50,000 in year one, in year 2, you'd take out $51,000, and so on. This is a simplification of a complicated study, but it's a super common rule of thumb to follow that helps you identify *how much is enough* to safely retire and safely withdraw in retirement.

I don't mean retire as in the traditional retirement age of 67. Once you hit your FI number, as long as you only live off of 4% of your portfolio annually, you won't run out of money (with a reasonable degree of certainty).

Step 3 Part 1: Calculate how much passive income (if any) you have and subtract that from your pre-25x FI number.

This step has two parts. Both are optional and may or may not apply to you. For part one, passive income reduces your FI number if you earn any. In other words, if you did quit your job where you traded time for money, how much money would still consistently continue to come in? Subtract that from your step 1 number.

I've monetized my YouTube channel, and I've self-published two books. I also have a finance course and earn some money through affiliate marketing and Medium. For you, that could be a blog you monetized, a podcast you started, or the most popular form of passive income: real estate. I do recommend you err on the side of caution, though, because it's hard to know if/when passive income streams could "dry up." My books could become bargain bin leftovers. YouTube could change the whole ad platform or algorithm. Podcasts could become replaced by Clubhouse or Twitter Spaces (or whatever is new these days)! Owning rental properties feels like the only safe passive income stream, but even that can be difficult to accurately predict as the housing market also fluctuates.

For the calculation, if your annual spending is $50,000, but you expect to earn $5,000 a year in passive income, you would multiply $45,000 by 25—your FI Number shifts from $1.25M to $1.125M in this scenario.

Step 3 Part 2: Reduce your current savings and investments from your FI number.

How do your current investments impact how long it will take you to reach FI? It's simple. Take your FI number; let's say it's now $1.125M, and subtract the money you have invested. If that's $125,000, you need $1 million. If you are able to save $50,000 a year, it will take you 20 years to get to FI. $1M / 50K is the equation. Again, take your FI number *minus* your investments, *divided by* your annual spending. The best way to do all of this is a FI calculator you can easily find online.

Summary

Here are the 3 steps to find your FI number:

1. Determine your annual expenses
2. Multiply that number by 25
3. Optional: Adjust your equation depending on the amount of passive income you expect to receive consistently and any money you already have invested.

FINAL THOUGHTS AND TAKEAWAYS

Do not react to the market once you have hit your FI number. Stay the course. As long as you have a built-up emergency fund, in a high-interest savings account, this shouldn't be difficult. I recommend you recalculate your FI number every 6 months to a year or anytime there's a dramatic shift in your life or lifestyle.

Your FI number is a general guideline to help you identify a goal. It is not a bulletproof plan or secret of the rich. Take it for what it is and harness the number to inspire and motivate you.

That's the what. Let's get back to the how, starting with a core mental block holding most people back.

Part II

FIRE Mentality

CHAPTER SIX

Conquer This Mental Hurdle To Increase Your Savings Rate

You have a financial thermostat that needs recalibrating

What is the point of making money? To do what with it? Is it to spend it? Is it to save it? You might be thinking I'm going to say the latter: to save it. I'm not. The point of money is freedom, choice, and opportunity. I don't look at money as a means to becoming rich monetarily. I look at it as being "time rich." Money is a tool that allows you to do what you want when you want, with whom you want to do it. That's how I define financial freedom. Those seeking financial independence, and even early retirement, is actually seeking financial freedom. Freedom of choice in life. Work. Travel. Start a business. It's all up to you.

That's what making money and saving money is all about. Freedom is my big "why" of money and saving it. It's why I aim to save and invest half of my income as a savings rate goal. If you don't find a way to break through and increase your savings rate and increase how much you invest, it's going to be very difficult to experience freedom in life. Your bank account is a representation of your freedom. It might sound a little extreme, but it's absolutely true. So, how do we increase our savings? How do we increase our freedom?

The Financial Thermostat

I first heard about this idea of *The Financial Thermostat* on Rob Dial's podcast The Mindset Mentor. It's a fantastic podcast. Here's how it works. Most people have a thermostat in their house. The purpose is to help you regulate the temperature in a room or throughout your home. A lot of people keep it at or around 70 degrees. When it gets too far away from 70 degrees, let's say 65 degrees, the heat will click back on and bring it back to 70 degrees. At 75 degrees, *CLICK* the A/C will turn on until it gets back to 70. You also have a financial thermostat, and it works the same way. Take a moment and reflect on these questions:

What number are you used to seeing in your savings account?
How about your checking account?
Your emergency fund?

It might be $500. It might be $5,000. For me, it was $3,000 in an emergency fund. For nearly 10 years, it sat at $3,000. Rarely more. Rarely less. The problem was, I didn't spend it when an emergency did occur. Instead, I swiped my credit card and accrued debt. Because of my financial thermostat, I preferred debt over seeing my emergency fund drop.

Whatever your number is, that's what has become comfortable for you. It's become your norm. Your sweet spot. Your comfort zone. Let me know if this sounds familiar: When you find yourself too far away from what you're used to seeing in your account, on either end, your behavior changes. If you have too little, you panic a bit.

Let's say you're hit with a big unexpected $500 or $1,000 bill. *Uh oh... holy crap. I gotta fix this. How do I recoup or replace those funds?* You think about your recent behavior and determine a path to get back on track. You cut out fast food. You make your own coffee daily. You work a few hours of overtime. You might say no to happy hour because you remember last time happy hour led to more bars after eating out and a $100 tab.

So, you likely either work extra or you cut back. In a month or so, you get back to where you were. Crisis averted. Back to comfort. Phew.

Problem solved… right? It happens in the opposite way as well when you get a tax return, a bonus check, or a raise. It happens when you pick up a side hustle and suddenly have a newfound surplus of funds in your account. What happens then?

CLICK

The thermostat turns on, and you spend it. That's extra money! Free cash. You earned it, after all. You have some savings, after all. Plus, the thing you want is on sale. And really, when was the last time you bought some clothes? You're in dire need of a wardrobe update. A phone upgrade. A new barbecue. Tickets to the game… This doesn't usually happen with one big purchase. It happens a bit more slowly over time—over a series of small, unnecessary purchases.

And I get it. I did the exact same thing for almost 10 years when it came to savings. I cut back when I fell behind. I stayed in on weekends. I picked up side gigs. Then I spent 100% of side gig money, and then some. But at least I had that $3,000… right? I bet a decent percentage of you reading this have been sitting right around the same amount for the last year in your savings or emergency fund. Maybe 5 years, 10 years, 15 years, or more. And now you know why. You have a financial thermostat. It's not conscious. It's subconscious. It's what you know. It's what feels comfortable.

FINAL THOUGHTS AND TAKEAWAYS

It's important to recognize your financial thermostat comfort zone when it comes to money saved in your checking, savings, or emergency fund. For some, understanding this idea and internalizing it could be enough to help you break through and save more. Others might be thinking, *Okay great. I get it. Makes sense. But how do I actually increase my savings rate in practice? Are there more concrete, tangible things I can do?* Absolutely! It's called goals. It's creating systems and automating your way to financial success. It's paying yourself first. Developing a money mentality and an abundance mindset is also a big part of it.

Now that you understand the financial thermostat, I hope you're thinking about how to crank the dial up permanently. Doing so will help you stay positive and motivated on your journey. I found the financial thermostat lesson to be so valuable, it's video Lesson 1 in Module 1 of my first online course "Save Money Resolution". It's 1 mini-lesson of 30+ over 7 modules. Enjoy a free preview of the course at www.TheMoneyResolution.com.

Did this concept make a light bulb *CLICK*? The financial thermostat is a small, but mighty idea to grasp. As you'll see ahead, stacking small concepts together can lead to huge wins!

CHAPTER SEVEN

Think Small to Achieve Big Savings Goals

Tiny thoughts. Huge results.

Are you ready for some small talk? I've been chewing on these tiny ideas for a while. I hope one or more really stands out and helps you think a little differently, a little smaller when it comes to saving more. Small mindset shifts can lead to serious gains!

Time

The problem with big savings goals is time. Researchers from the University of Pennsylvania found that the longer you pursue a goal, the farther away it seems, which can lead you to get sidetracked or give up—even if you're close to reaching your goal. Not knowing when the goal is going to arrive is a key contributing factor. An example is calling customer service and being put on hold. You hope and think it'll be 30 seconds but after 5 minutes you give up. Ugh. The longer you wait, the longer you think you'll have to wait. It may sound counterintuitive, but it's true.

If your savings goal is too big or going to take too long, you may be setting yourself up to fail and you'll be more likely to give up or give in to temptations. Instead, set a specific end date to make the goal as concrete and specific as possible. It'll make it much easier to stick with it and stay motivated.

That said, I recognize you can't set shorter timeframes for some of your goals. For example, retirement might be a decade or two or three away. Most of us simply stash away and invest a portion of our 401(k) each paycheck without thinking about it. Instead, sit down and run your retirement numbers. You might be surprised by what you find out. Learn how to optimize your 401(k) by watching my YouTube video "5 Best Ways to Optimize Your 401(k) Today!"

Running numbers through a retirement calculator is what led me to the goal of early retirement. After crunching different numbers, I realized if I saved and invested 35% of my income or more (post-tax), I could retire a decade sooner. I could retire 2 decades sooner if I was able to get my savings rate to 50%.

17 years was a long way off when I got started, but that made it more attainable and realistic. I genuinely feel most day-to-day financial decisions I make are connected to this more tangible and less far-off goal of early retirement.

Smaller goals

It's important to break big goals into smaller, obtainable goals. Retirement was 17 years away, but I know how much I need to save and invest each year to get me to that goal. Now it's a game to move that end date even sooner. I started side hustling and reinvesting in myself to see bigger returns someday. Ideally, I can bank and reinvest most of those returns for bigger returns and so on.

Think about your life and your goals. First of all, do you set and track financial goals? If not, start there but again, think small. What can you stash away for Future You this year? What does that look like monthly? What does that look like weekly or even daily? Saving $10,000 in a year doesn't seem nearly as difficult when you realize that's $833 a month. That's $192 a week. It's a tick over $27 a day. Great. Can you now cut $27 in expenses? Maybe not at first, but eventually? Abso-freaking-lutely!

This smaller goal concept is actually an effective idea. A recent study published in Psychological Science found that people who break down their savings goals into smaller time frames, like weeks or months, save 78% more money than people who solely focus on a far-off future goal. It's legitimately true so give it a real shot.

If you think small and set incremental victory checkpoints, it's important you check in on your bigger picture goals often. It's motivating to see your progress and might offer a good opportunity to course-correct and adjust if needed.

I started at -$80,000 in 2018. I set a small goal to pay off my credit cards. My next goal was to get to net worth zero. Before I knew it, I accomplished my third goal of 6-figures positive in early 2021. My new goal is to hit $250,000 by the end of 2022. I fully understand and appreciate the power of small goals.

Personal Capital

Speaking of net worth, if you want a full picture of your financial health and net worth, I suggest you connect any and all accounts—your assets and your liabilities—to Personal Capital to easily track your net worth over time. This connects to all of my accounts including savings accounts, credit cards, loans, my HSA, and more seamlessly and updates fast. I've been using and getting value out of Personal Capital for years as it's become my go-to for tracking my net worth. They also offer banking services, retirement tools, investing overviews with great insights, and an excellent blog. It's my favorite financial service because it has all the tools in one and it's totally free. I highly recommend you sign up and start getting value from it as I do. It only requires a *small* effort to get started.

Keep your main bank account low

I've never heard anyone talk about this strategy but it's one I employ that might work for you. I like to keep my personal savings and checking accounts low. It means that every dollar is being put to work. I set up automation so my money gets transferred to my investing app weekly and invested automatically. I pay bills and credit cards automatically. I also manually move what I can to an external online-only bank account with Ally for savings. I like living on the edge financially in this sense. It's a constant reminder that money is tight. This helps me resist splurges. It's a psychological trick that works for me. Either way remember, money sitting in a standard bank account is losing money due to inflation, so put that money to work. Consider trying out this smaller bucket approach with your main savings account. That said, I wouldn't recommend it without a safety net built up.

Save using the 80/20 rule

The 80/20 rule means that 20% of your actions yield 80% of the results. Leverage the 80/20 rule to save more money. You could cut 20% of your spending that could lead to 80% of new savings. Let's discuss the less obvious first:

- Eating out isn't too expensive. The drinks and desserts are, so cut those.
- Vacations aren't expensive. The hotels, transportation, and souvenirs are. Find a way to reduce those line items with discounts or travel points. For souvenirs, maybe take pictures of actual souvenirs or develop your own postcard which is way cheaper and much more rewarding since you DIY'd it.
- Going to a sporting event isn't expensive. The beers, hotdogs, new jersey, and parking are.
- Attending a friend's house party isn't expensive. The new shirt and fancy wine you arrive with to impress the host are.

See what parts of your fun cost you the most and try to reduce or eliminate them. In addition, learn to say no to some of the events some of the time. Resist temptations and add ons. I leverage credit card points to make vacations more affordable. I create a mental spending limit when I go to a sporting event or attend a party. I even bring food to baseball games and the movies. It's not cheap or illegal. It's smart.

The obvious way I could have taken the 80/20 rule is to focus on reducing your biggest expenses. For most, that's your housing, food, and transportation. If you focus on reducing this chunk of your spending, you can save more and worry less about day-to-day expenses.

Incremental increases matter

In your quest for financial independence, small increases in savings and investing can help you make big strides. For example, if you increase your retirement savings by 1% or $100 each month, you'll hardly notice the difference, but that might grow tens of thousands more in the long run. Giving yourself a raise is critical. You should absolutely give yourself a raise when you earn a raise. Bank any and all increases in pay including bonuses. Invest it and enjoy years shaved off of your working life.

Stash every cent

I first heard about an app called Acorns in early 2018 and decided to give it a go. You can connect your debit card and Acorns will automatically round up your spending and send those extra coins to Acorns where they invest it. I liked stashing $30 to $50 a month aside without noticing. But I wanted more. With Acorns, you can 2x, 3x, or 4x those round-ups. Plus, I adjust my rules so that purchases ending with $.00 moved a full dollar over. Finally, I connected my credit cards and did the same as my debit card. There is a small fee ($3 a month) to use the service, but I do recommend it for young people, or anyone getting started with savings goals.

Pro tip: Save every $5 bill you come across. It doesn't matter when, where, or why. If you ever come in possession of $5, put it in a jar. Period. You might be shocked how much this small effort leads to big savings!

FINAL THOUGHTS AND TAKEAWAYS

I covered the importance of setting shorter time-bound goals to keep you motivated. One way to do this is by breaking down large goals into smaller chunks. Either way, it starts with a goal-setting exercise and tracking your net worth. Then I took the *think small* concept further and talked about having a smaller amount of money in the bank account you check most often, so you aren't tempted to spend when you're heavy on cash flow.

Next, I discussed the 80/20 rule and focused on the 20% of your actions that make the biggest difference when it comes to saving money. Finally 3 quick tips: The first was small incremental increases in saving you'll hardly notice, as well as the fact that every penny counts, especially if you use a service like Acorns. Plus, I shared my $5 pro tip—always bank those Lincolns! That's a lot of small talk. It's time for a game-changing big idea most people need to hear…

CHAPTER EIGHT

The Real Reason People Are Bad With Money

"They say ignorance is bliss... they're wrong" -Franz Kafka

If you're part of the roughly half of Americans who can't come up with $2,000 in 30 days for an emergency, this is for you. If you're not sure how to get started with tackling debt or your finances in general, this is for you. Even if you already think you're a finance ninja, this is for you because you'll see how there are layers to this big idea that applies to everyone. The fact is, we all have room for improvement when it comes to personal finance. At the end of this chapter, I'll offer 5 concrete solutions to overcome the problem. What is that problem?

The Ostrich Effect

The real reason people are bad with money is because of the ostrich effect. According to The Decision Lab: "The ostrich effect describes how people often avoid negative information, including feedback that could help them monitor their goal progress. Instead of dealing with the situation, we bury our heads in the sand, like ostriches. This avoidance can often make things worse, incurring costs that we might not have had to pay if we had faced things head-on."

Originally, it was coined based on attempts by investors to avoid negative financial information due to fear of negative performance. Studies show that investors check their portfolios far more often when the market is up than when the market is down. This is a psychological response to what we know to be bad news. It's human nature to avoid information that can be upsetting.

Blind success

Funny enough, keeping your head in the sand altogether is a good strategy when it comes to investing. I always recommend investing in index funds that track either the S&P 500 or the total stock market and investing a set amount, at a set time interval, no matter what. This is called dollar-cost averaging. Ignore the market completely. Set it and forget it. Stay the course. In the long run, the market always goes up.

I've developed an aversion to receiving all real-time investing information, especially information about a down market because those losses are temporary. People often forget you don't lock in losses unless you sell investments when they're down. Understanding historical performance (again, it always goes up over time) is all you need to know to feel confident going forward.

The market took a huge downturn in 2009 when the housing market crashed. Smart long-term investors knew to avoid the news and fear-inducing headlines. If you're investing for the long-term, it's best to not get caught up in the weeds of day-to-day volatility. Burying your head in the sand can be good for this one specific reason.

Otherwise, the head-in-the-sand syndrome is real and damaging financially. It's so real, people probably put their head in the sand to avoid this reality!

Psychological discomfort

The definition of the ostrich effect has widened and is commonly used in reference to people that avoid exposing themself to negative information in fear of it causing psychological discomfort. Many people hide information or ignore problems because the truth can hurt. It is human nature to run away from threats or fear the unknown. This happens often in real life in many ways. For example:

- Avoiding the doctor or dentist

- Developing anxiety about an upcoming performance review
- Avoiding the scale even when you're on a weight loss program
- Not knowing the annual interest rates on your credit cards like half of Americans

Don't mistake these for laziness. It's in our DNA to avoid difficult situations and bad news. We despise losing. Instead, we protect our ego by staying firm in our happy-go-lucky beliefs.

Wile E. Coyote is the poster child for avoiding the truth. Whenever he finds himself outwitted by that darn roadrunner, he'll often admit defeat by doing something like covering his eyes when he's staring at a train barreling down on him with dynamite on the tracks. We laugh and sympathize because we can relate. But his situations, like many of life's bad situations, are avoidable. Ignorance is bliss. But it's still ignorance.

The reason most people are bad with money is that they don't understand their financial situation *because* they avoid it. They don't log into their accounts. They don't track spending or net worth. They don't set goals. People hide from reality. They bury their heads in the sand. Then they wonder how their debt reached 5-figures. They fail to understand that ignoring the problem is robbing their future selves. Plus, they're missing out on the benefit of time *in* the market.

Time can be your best friend or your worst enemy. Compound interest is great when you're invested and your money is growing exponentially. But time is a jerk when compound interest is working against you—like credit card interest or a pile of student loan debt.

I ignored my finances until January 1st, 2018. In the back of my mind, I knew it was bad but decided to deal with it later. I did, but it took years of commitment to dig myself out of a hole to make up for decades of lost time and poor decisions. I'm proof you technically can deal with it later. That said, I missed out on years and years of investment growth I'll never get back. I don't dwell on it anymore (what's done is done, let it go), but I recognize my early retirement could have been now, not age 45 or 50 in the future had I faced my fears a decade ago.

Excuses

Getting organized is hard. Knowing your net worth or credit score can sound terrifying. Learning about investing? I'd rather get a root canal. It doesn't help that talking about money has become incredibly taboo. Most of us feel like we have nobody to talk to about money. We don't know who to trust. We feel alone and embarrassed. Plus, they didn't teach this stuff in school! But these are excuses. I eventually found that out the hard way. You don't have to.

This ostrich effect is holding people back, putting people in debt, and it gets far worse when ignored. It also affects people that are decent with money but could be even better. We all have blind spots. We all have room for improvement. Most people aren't preparing for their future. The data doesn't lie. 63% of people are living paycheck to paycheck in the United States. Some studies indicate this number is higher. It's not all doom and gloom. The alternative is simple. *Don't* deal with it later. Get started today.

Where to start

First of all, get financially prepared for emergencies! Setting aside $1,000 that you will only touch when an emergency comes up is a massive step and will help you sleep better at night. Because as Mike Tyson famously said, "Everybody has a plan until they get punched in the mouth." If you've made mistakes or have regrets, let them go. Take it one day and one action item at a time. There is nothing more relieving than knowing that you took that first positive step in the right direction.

Next, invest more towards retirement. Time is your best friend when it comes to investing. A 10% return for 20 years generates more money than a 20% return for 10 years. Plus, not contributing towards a company match is throwing away free money. Become aware. Take action. Automate your way to financial success.

You don't know what you don't know

The ostrich effect means people continue to not know what they don't know. This is called the Dunning-Kruger effect, where people lack enough basic financial knowledge to even realize that they're making mistakes. People's lack of understanding about key concepts like compound interest and inflation can lead to thinking you're making good financial decisions when you're making things worse. Further ignoring finances can lead to succumbing to "lifestyle creep" where your spending increases as your income rises. Some might call that a good problem to have but no, it's a problem. As you earn more, you should absolutely save and invest more — not get better at spending.

A recent study showed 18% of people earning 6-figures are still living paycheck to paycheck. By spending money as they get it, they're stealing from their future selves. People also develop bad money habits that stick, like impulse buying. As an example, they congratulate themselves for saving $20 on a pair of $100 jeans instead of admitting they splurged away $80. Because of the ostrich effect, people would rather feel good about saving than look closely at their spending.

How to overcome the Ostrich Effect

Ignoring personal finances is bad, obviously. But what's good? Here are non-obvious strategies to help you overcome head-in-the-sand syndrome:

Develop mindfulness

Being aware of the problem is step one. Ask yourself some challenging personal questions like "What am I really afraid of?" or my favorite: "If I were giving my friend advice about the same situation, what advice would I give them?"

For the first question, you might surprise yourself with what you come up with. It could be fear of the unknown. Fear of failure. Fear of feeling helpless. Fear of damaging your ego. There's usually something else beneath the surface causing the issue. And you would *never* tell a friend to ignore their financial situation so why would you do it yourself? The friend perspective offers instant personal perspective.

Get exposed

The exposure effect is real and it means that things become more likable as we expose ourselves to them more often. Taking 5 minutes a day to look your financial fears in the face or confront a blind spot is an excellent starting point. You might find the situation isn't as bad as you thought. You might also find a few quick wins that help you build momentum. Then, gamify it. See how many days in a row you can spend 15 minutes working on your finances as a goal. Celebrate in a fiscally responsible way when you break a record.

Getting exposed means replacing imagination with real-life data consistently. Force yourself to look. It's the best way to conquer fear. It's like being convinced there's a monster under your bed as a kid. The first time you looked it was extreme relief. The 10th time you looked was the last time you believed in monsters. And by you I mean me...

Develop a long-term mindset

When trying to improve your financial life, or even trying to scale your investments, know that you will experience setbacks. That's okay when you have a long-term mindset. Turning a bad financial situation around is going to take time. Completing goals takes time. Building wealth or starting a business takes time.

The same is true when losing weight. It's consistent action with a long-term approach that dictates a successful result. And as hard and challenging as things can feel in the moment, I like to picture myself in the future looking back on the journey with extreme satisfaction. This is also a good time to establish *why* you're doing something. Why do you want to improve your financial situation? What would it mean to succeed? Don't be in a hurry. That will get overwhelming, fast.

Help yourself or ask for help

Admit that you don't know what you don't know and get started by getting educated. This could actually be your first action. Start learning. It's a beautifully simple first step.

That's what I did in my year of getting good with money in 2018. I found a finance podcast I loved and previously mentioned: The Stacking Benjamins Show. I listened to it every day. Eventually, I had a few "ah-ha" moments that propelled me into action. I wasn't expecting that but learning encouraged me to overcome my fear.

The second thing I did was get a library card and put a dozen finance books on hold. There are many free resources available, but it has to come from a genuine place of curiosity. And here is a quick tip about reading: don't read because completion is the goal. Read to learn. Read chapters out of order. Take notes in the margins (unless it's a library book!). Either way, get curious and get knowledgeable.

Automate

A really nice and easy way to get started is to automate your bill payments so you won't miss a payment and get hit with a fee. You can also automate your savings. Increase your work retirement contribution by 1% or commit to setting aside $100 into savings as soon as you get started. It's like hiring a personal trainer—you commit financially so that you *know* you'll show up to the (finance) gym.

I've also found ways to automatically make time for learning throughout my day. When I take the dog for a walk, exercise, or [insert chore here], I use that time to listen to an educational podcast or audiobook. What's great about automation is that it's a beautiful foundation to build on. Most of my financial wins happen automatically. I wrote books and started a finance YouTube channel because I kept wanting to work on my finances, but there was only so much I could do daily once I automated almost everything.

Talk to an accountability partner

I do this with my wife during what we call "Money Parties" once a month. You can ask family or even a close friend for help or advice. You can seek out a professional. You can even contact work. You might be surprised about how willing HR is to point you in the right direction. Either way, open up about your situation and talk to somebody.

FINAL THOUGHTS AND TAKEAWAYS

Honestly, I struggled to write and finish this chapter. I spent days researching. I started over 3 different times because I had the opposite issues: too much information which leads to analysis paralysis.

At one point I buried my head in the sand and put it out of sight and out of mind for a few days. Ultimately I committed and overcame my personal doubts and fears. Push forward with positivity and confidence. Take it one day at a time. That helped me finally pull through to finish this. It's okay to be vulnerable and admit to struggling or needing help.

We all have blind spots — fears that hold us back or gaps in education. We all have things that keep us up at night. I call these mental monsters. I challenge you to continue to think about the money things you don't know or the parts of your financial life you ignore. I challenge you to overcome the ostrich effect.

Focus on doing what you've been avoiding. Learn about challenging financial topics you've been avoiding. Focus on bringing light to your financial fears and self-improvement. Getting stronger in an area of strength is good. But if you can turn your weakness into a strength, you will be *great*. Possibly, unstoppable.

If it's all dark and dim because you avoid all things money (like many), get started. Make the commitment. The first step is the hardest. But remember, only an object in motion can gain momentum. If you stick with it, you'll discover success comes gradually, then suddenly.

We all hate loss and losing, but ignoring a problem or financial issues is the only guaranteed way to lose. The only thing you have to fear is fear itself. If nothing else, remember this: Ignorance isn't bliss. It's ignorance. Curiosity is king and knowledge is power. Every day you're moving forwards or backward financially. Get your head out of the sand and move forward today.

Then, take flight!

CHAPTER NINE

You Need This Much By Age To Retire...

End this exercise. There's a better way to define financial success

There are countless pieces of information out there on the internet telling you the *correct* way to calculate how much money you need to retire and at what age. To be completely frank and brutally honest, *it's mostly bullshit.* Let me explain AND offer an actionable approach you can start implementing today instead.

First off, I'm not out to criticize anyone who simply wants to know where they stand compared to their peers. If you have no idea, turn to the data and, so to speak, "experts." After all, there's more information available to us for free now than ever, so take advantage of it.

As a caveat, there are multiple warnings that you should know. One of which is information overload. Information overload can be a real thing, especially if the information makes you feel bad, which is inherently what's going to happen here. The data shows most Americans are behind and off-track when it comes to the traditional retirement age. Yet, it's human nature to want and compare ourselves to one another. In fact, the #1 question people ask financial advisors is: *How am I doing compared to other clients?*

I'm not sure why we have this tendency to compare. Maybe it's some sort of survival instinct from days long gone. We do it all the time, and most of the time, we do it unconsciously. This does a lot of harm and damage. Let's cover why you need to be aware of it and reasonable solutions to help you avoid this comparison thinking—

which spirals into negative thinking, self-doubt, regret, and maybe even the 5 stages of grief…

Before I get started, I want to start with actionable financial real-life money advice I wish I knew many, many years ago:

If you're only saving money, you're doing it wrong.

Most articles say, "Here's how much you need *saved…*" but that alone is misleading. You cannot save your way to retirement alone. **You must invest.** It isn't about earning more or spending less. It's about how you set up your money to earn more money. You can trade-in your time for money or you can make sure your money is always working for you. This was my biggest miss financially growing up. After college, I avoided investing for a decade because it seemed scary. It really isn't and doesn't have to be.

My second key piece of financial advice is: If your salary increases, your savings should proportionally increase as well. As people earn more, they typically get better at spending. Annual expenses go up. Savings rates go down. If that's the case, no matter how much money you have saved, you are delaying retirement if you allow this to happen. As your spending increases (and therefore your annual expenses rise), you suddenly need to save and invest more to retire on time if you want to afford your new, more expensive, or comfortable lifestyle in retirement.

In some cases, the amount of retirement income needed could double or triple. Let's be real, the majority of people cannot build a nest egg of $1 million dollars. Frankly, if you found out from one of these articles or a retirement calculator that's how much you need, you'll want to give up. *It's laughable. Why even try?*

This brings up a very important point about the "how much you need saved by age" conversation. There is no fool-proof way to measure if you're off track or ahead of the game. There are *far* too many variables to consider to give anybody end-all-be-all evergreen advice.

- Are you married?

- Do you have kids?
- Do you already own a home? If so, how much of the mortgage is paid?
- Do you have debts?
- Where do you live?
- At what age are you starting your FIRE journey?
- What kind of retirement will you have?
- How will your investment do?
- Will you need long-term health care?

The list goes on and on...

However, clickbait articles and YouTube videos on the topic typically do a lot more harm than good. Those articles and videos with definitive numbers simply end up making you feel *worthless*, quite literally. They're dreadful reminders about mistakes you've made in the past. That is never how I approach personal finance. In fact, the first unofficial tip in the introduction of my second book is this:

Forgive Yourself. Stop beating yourself up for mistakes you've made or procrastination that has delayed your success. You won't be able to focus on the future if you spend energy thinking about the past. Start fresh, think forward, and stay positive. Mindset is everything. Rather than focusing on a retirement formula first with unlimited variables, you should focus instead on these 3 steps no matter where you are financially and at any age:

Step 1: *Take a step back and focus on what age you want to retire.*

Don't be scared to dream big and try to retire early even if you feel "way behind." You know what they say about aiming for the moon and landing amongst the stars, right?

Step 2: *Evaluate what type of retirement you hope to have.*

If it's traveling or otherwise lavish, you've got some serious work to do. If it's the opposite and you can keep expenses low, you might be able to retire in 15 or 20 years no matter where you're at now, even with a savings rate below 50%.

Step 3: Build habits before you focus on numbers or vague rules of thumb or guidelines.

Like getting fit, working on your financial muscles takes consistent habits over time. You build habits day by day. If you feel behind or off track, you will *not* fix it with sheer will and force one day or even in one month.

With that said, let's discuss a critical mental concept I learned about from the Financial Rockstar podcast: Gap Mentality vs. Gain Mentality.

I'm going to start by sharing the data most articles and videos cover—how much you technically should have saved by age to retire on time. Take a moment to study the chart below. It represents how much you and/or your partner needs saved by age if your salary or combined salary equaled $125,000 annually. Pretend these were your numbers. Then face the numbers for a moment and digest them:

**Assumes 2 household incomes totaling $125,000*

Age	Amount needed	Total
25	Half	$62,500
30	1x	$125,000
35	2x	$250,000
40	3x	$375,000
45	4x	$500,000
50	5x	$625,000
55	6x	$750,000
60	7x	$875,000
65	8x	$1,000,000

Source: Investopedia

I bet I know the first thing you did—you located your age. You locked in on the closest line, and you compared it to your own estimated net worth or savings. That's normal. As you looked at those numbers, you were likely measuring yourself in the gap, not the gain. As you looked at these numbers, did you think: *I feel behind?* That right there is gap thinking. It's looking to compare yourself to the status quo. Instead, I suggest you work on developing gain thinking. Think about the progress you've made. Think about where you were 5, 10, 20 years ago and where you are today. What have you gained? How far have you come? And what opportunity lies ahead of you? (Hint: I'm not only talking about money.)

If you're saving for a down payment on a house, don't think to yourself, *I'm still $30,000 away*. Instead, shift this thinking to *Wow, 18* *months ago, I had $5,000 saved. Now I have $12,000. I've more than doubled it.* I'm making numbers up, but you get the idea. Typically, money breeds gap thinking. It creates little success scorecards. It's dangerous, it's unhealthy, and it's never productive.

To practice gain thinking or gain mentality, remember that money is simply a tool. It's neutral. It's your peers and the media that make it seem like more than that. Money helps you get what you want. It's that simple. Everyone is different. Minimalists need very little. Some want a lot and have a desire to travel often. You can only compare yourself to your *future* needs and wants out of life. Better yet, compare yourself to where you were 10 years ago financially and from a happiness perspective.

Here's another interesting point about gap thinkers: they can be extremely successful but not necessarily happy. They continue to move the goalposts to want more and more, and/or they spend the bulk of their time working because of #hustleculture. They don't stop to reflect on what matters most, who matters most, what they really want out of life, or their big picture *why*. If you want to be unhappy, compare yourself to others. If you want to be happy, spend time reflecting on where you are now vs. where you used to be. Spend time thinking about where you want to be in the future and why. Catch yourself when you find yourself admiring the Joneses, thinking about what others think of you, or comparing yourself to others in general. Those mental exercises are toxic and limiting.

Gain thinking can benefit you in many ways beyond personal finance. For example, I wanted to start a blog for years. Finally, I figured out, the only thing holding me back was fear of what others would think and comparison to those that are much more successful than me.

Then I redefined success for the *Future Me*. If I can gain 100 followers on Medium, that would be awesome. If I can learn how to earn money from writing daily, that would be amazing. If I can write three articles a week instead of one, I could help and reach more people with my message. If I can show up consistently, I would be proud of that. Since then, every day my metrics look a tiny bit better. I'm able to reach more people because of my habits—all because I developed gain thinking.

I often think to myself, *where will I be 10 years from now if I keep working as hard as I am now, with the same positive attitude I have now? Where will I be if I get 1% better each day?* You will never be at the top. That's okay. There will always be somebody smarter, better, stronger, younger, prettier, richer, and so on than you. Or retired sooner than you, and that's great!

Live your life with a focus on what matters most. I personally think good financial knowledge and money can help get you there, but if you think money alone gets you there, you're missing the point. Run your own race. **Comparison is the root of all unhappiness.** Your story is uniquely yours and different is better than better.

Never let articles or benchmarks from supposed experts tell you how to live your life. **It is NEVER too late to change your financial life** or radically change your life in general. If you feel bad about your current situation, now is the perfect time to say out loud: *"I can't wait to be an anomaly and retire early anyways!"*

Get determined. Stay positive. Build gain thinking and build good habits. Small efforts day in and day out will show you the way.

Plus, of course, I explained a truly reliable way to calculate your FIRE number in Chapter 5: "How to Calculate Your FIRE Number" which will help you with clarity and defining goals.

CHAPTER TEN

7 Unexpected Ways to Gain Financial Clarity

How to underthink big decisions, unlock your growth mindset, and have your best year ever.

Black swan events is a term in the financial space where a negative cataclysmic event occurs and no one was expecting it. COVID-19 not only had a profound impact on society's health, but everyone's personal finance changed forever. According to Bankrate, 42% of households said incomes are still below pre-pandemic levels. In mid-December 2020, more than 60% of Americans reported they were likely to fall short of their annual financial goals.

How does one pull themself out of those deficits, adapt, and become more resilient than ever? It starts with the mind and clarity before rushing into drastic action. Your mindset leads to clarity. Clarity is about eliminating doubt and mystery about what you should be doing next. I'm hoping you can take on clarity as a state of existence. And that mental state of clarity leads to positive, consistent action.

Let's get creative. Let's get real and honest for a bit. Maybe even controversial. Let's unlock our growth mindset together by tapping into how we think and how we should think about our money. Here are unexpected ways to gain financial clarity this year and beyond:

Understand that money is a tool and wealth is just a game

Money is a neutral tool. It doesn't do anything until you use it and do something with it. It's important to know that it is not inherently good or evil. Examining your relationship with money should start here. Some lose clarity because they see money as a major stress in their life and nothing more. You have to earn it, protect it, grow it, spend it wisely, and the list goes on. Yes, that's a lot to get your head around, and it's persistent in our daily lives. But, when you shift your thinking and start to see money as a tool, a useful tool, it can change your mentality and increase your motivation.

Don't let money become the sole purpose of your life. I assure you, you'll never have enough if you keep chasing more. Instead, think about how you can use the tool to get what you want and where you want to go. A great way to do this is to focus on spending your money on anything that will aid your growth. Use one tool to sharpen another. It would be an interesting exercise to look back at your last 30 days of spending and put a checkmark or an X next to each line item after deciding if it aided your growth or not. Did money as a tool help you learn something new, get closer to your goals, perform better in your job, or become a better partner in a relationship?

You can also use money as a tool to buy your time. Perhaps that's hiring a maid once a week. Or, on a large scale, as in saving aggressively now so you can retire 5, 10, or 15 years sooner than the average person. If you determine you're underspending on growth and buying time, but overspending on short-term pleasures, perhaps you're doing it wrong. Instead, use money to buy personal growth and your time back.

I also mentioned wealth is just a game. Don't take it too seriously and know the rules of the game. Like sharpening an ax, sharpening your knowledge and financial literacy can be more lucrative long-term than that new side hustle you're considering. More on this in a moment.

Develop a self-care money mentality

To find more clarity around your money, build it into your self-care daily routine. Every day we brush our teeth, shower, get some fresh air, plan our meals, and sometimes choose organic because it's better for us. You might stretch, journal, meditate or take a long bath on Sunday nights to wind down. Perhaps you always aim to get a good night's sleep.

It's time you look at your financial health as equally important as your physical and mental health. For starters, think about how many minutes or hours a week you exercise. Now think about how many minutes or hours a week you work on your personal finances. Could you make that one and the same?

Earlier, I encouraged you to work on your finances for 1% of your day. That's 14 minutes and 24 seconds. I challenged you to do this for 30 days straight. That's because I believe it goes beyond a challenge. It's about building habits. Variety is the spice of life, so don't work on your finances by making a payment on your credit card or pretending to "crunch some numbers." Write down your goals or update them. Read a finance book. Assign beneficiaries or create a will. Set up a password manager for your account logins. Track your income. Up your retirement contribution. Rebalance your investments. Set up automated savings. Create an annual planner.

Don't get overwhelmed thinking there's so much to do. Tackle one small thing a day, for less than 15 minutes a day, and you'll quickly find that your actions will compound over time. Your return on this time will be exponentially more than the effort you put in.

Set exciting, smarter goals

You've probably heard of SMART goals. If I were to dive into that now, I would elicit many eye-rolls. Instead, I'm here to share a fresh take on setting SMART goals borrowed from Michael Hyatt's book Your Best Year Ever. Section 7 is called "Great Goals Check 7 Boxes." He changes several letters in the SMART acronym and adds an ER. Those stand for *exciting* and *relevant*.

For "exciting" he wrote: "*Researchers say that we stand a better chance of reaching our goals if we are internally motivated to do so. External motivations might work for a while, but if we're not getting something intrinsic from the goal, we'll lose interest.*" In terms of goals, he goes on to say: "*Go with what excites you. If you don't find your goals personally compelling, you won't have the motivation to push through when things get tough or tedious. This is where you've got to be honest with yourself."*

As yourself: Does this goal inspire me? Does it engage my heart? Am I willing to work hard to make it happen? Do I find it fun?

"Relevant" can help you ground your goals and path. It's an opportunity to reflect. He wrote, *"I look at this as a necessary gut-check. Before you commit to your goals, you must review them and ensure that they are taking into account your life circumstances as well as your values. What you hope to achieve this year must be balanced with the reality of your circumstances."*

It's easy to get off the path and get distracted if your goals aren't exciting and relevant.

Throw a Money Party!

Sounds fun, doesn't it? It is! Money parties have been one of my secret weapons to wealth building and planning. I've had many money parties with my partner, and this is a concept I really hope more people will try out. Money parties are really simple. It's a glorified money meeting. Once a month (at least), we pick an evening to talk about money and put it on the calendar. The key difference is we view it as a date night. It's essentially an at-home happy hour. We even do it on a Friday or Saturday night. We make fun drinks. We bring delicious snacks. And we don't feel bad about spending money to do so. We come together to talk about money in a super open, honest, and non-judgemental way.

We learned it's really important to land on a topic or theme ahead of time. This ensures the conversation stays on topic, and we can prepare ahead of time if we decide to. Yes, that sounds a little like homework, but picture having a party for completing your homework. Worth it.

One money party was all about setting our annual budget plan together. In order to do that, we each researched prior year spending by category. We came prepared with last year's numbers which made it much easier to project current year spending.

I recommend a few ground rules up front. We made a rule that anytime one of us was feeling like it was veering into stressful territory, we took a pause, said cheers, took a sip of our drinks, and either moved forward or went a different direction. It certainly helps us get clear in our personal goals and couple goals.

Work for passion OR work for money

I believe in knowing your why of life and your why of money. I believe in finding your passion and purpose in life. But here's a twist on that: Know your why as it pertains to your job and how you view your work. Here's what I mean. Ask yourself this: *Do you work for money or purpose? Or both?*

A recent survey found that people who said they work for money *and* purpose make less money than those who work for purpose *or* money alone.

The same survey revealed that people who worked for purpose in the spirit of helping earned more than those working for money. That's a head-scratcher, right? I bet many of you feel you work for both. It almost seems odd to exclusively work for money or purpose. If you simply want to accumulate wealth, you might find yourself eventually unfulfilled or worse, earning money at the expense of others. People who work exclusively to help others still need a roof over their heads, food on the table, and the necessities of life. Here's a possible explanation: perhaps people who work to earn money and work a meaningful, purpose-driven job, have a lack of clarity in terms of what motivates them most. As the great Ron Swanson famously said, "Never half-ass two things, whole ass one thing."

Leading with a desire to do good and follow a passion first is the real unlock to true, meaningful wealth. I suspect that a caring, kind person who thinks of others first might be better at keeping money and growing it. Often, people who want to earn money, only want to spend money.

This isn't black and white but it does make you think. The two motivations can conflict with one another. If you want true clarity in terms of your work and motivation, ponder this one a bit and be honest with yourself. What matters more to you: making money OR working for a purpose? What does that look like going forward?

Underthink it when it comes to investing and other difficult money decisions

When it comes to money, and especially investing, analysis paralysis is a real thing. But oftentimes, overanalyzing keeps you on the sidelines, falling behind and unclear about what to do next.

Earlier I said to view money as a game for perspective. If that's the case, know the basic rules. Now I'll add: don't play the game scared. Don't play recklessly, but jump in and participate. You'll win some. You'll lose some. It's just money. It's a tool. And you'll learn a tremendous amount along the way. Always remember, perfect is the enemy of good. It never feels like the exact right time to jump into the market. That's why you should dollar-cost average. We make bad decisions when we're emotional. Money is emotional. Make money unemotional by taking your decision-making out of it. Invest a specific amount at a specific time each month.

If you contribute to a retirement account at work, you're already dollar-cost averaging without thinking about it. Next, set up automation and do the same to max out a traditional or Roth IRA. I personally do this via M1 Finance to max out my Roth IRA each year.

Stop allotting yourself more time and take action. Go forward. Be decisive. Act with confidence even if you're not yet. You gain confidence and clarity with experience. And if you ever feel totally stuck, pause and learn a basic understanding or move on to the next thing. Move onto something that gets you excited. Life is too short to doubt yourself and be inactive.

"Don't put off until tomorrow, what you can do today" -Benjamin Franklin

FINAL THOUGHTS AND TAKEAWAYS

2020 was a year of change. 2022 and beyond is your time to adapt and become more resilient than ever by seeking clarity and adopting a growth mindset. Make this your year to get more clear than ever with financial goals, beliefs, and habits. Because financial freedom ultimately begins with clarity. If you aren't clear, if you don't have a why and the proper mindset, you won't achieve your what—no matter how exciting it seemed at first. Seek clarity and growth to discover financial freedom.

CHAPTER ELEVEN

The Wealth Snowball

The reverse of the debt snowball is a game-changer

I first heard of the wealth snowball while listening to the Afford Anything podcast, hosted by Paula Pant. In the episode, she interviewed JD Roth, of Get Rich Slowly fame, who shared the strategy. Shortly after, Paula chimed in with a different version of the wealth snowball. Both of their ideas are great strategies for growing your wealth. Before we tackle the wealth snowball, it's good to understand where the original idea came from: The Debt Snowball.

The Debt Snowball

The debt snowball is a debt payoff strategy where you take all of your debts and organize them from the lowest balance due to the highest. For example, if you had 3 credit cards with balances of $1,500, $500, and $1,000, you would reorganize them to $500, $1,000, and $1,500. From there, you go all-in on paying off the lowest debt while also paying the minimum on the other balances. While it might not make the most mathematical sense because you're ignoring interest rates, it can give you a psychological boost to see a debt get wiped out completely. Example results: wipe out your lowest debt which is $500. That's not too difficult and only takes a handful of weeks! The next debt is $1,000. That's not too hard either but takes more time. Finally, the $1,500 is the toughest, but since I already wiped out the first two debts with consistency, this too shall be erased!

The Wealth Snowball

The wealth snowball is somewhat of a reverse of the debt snowball. Essentially, JD's definition of the wealth snowball is to front-load investments so they can grow and compound. As long as you've paid off your debts, or at least the bad consumer ones like credit cards or a car note, go all-in on investing. Ideally, you'd start with your tax-advantaged retirement accounts like a work-sponsored 401(k) or your own IRA such as a Traditional or Roth IRA.

Why? It's because of the power of compound interest where the money your investment earns, also earns money and so on from there. It's the idea that it's time IN the market, not timing the market, that matters most. Another way of looking at this is, if you spend the next 2 years paying off your debt, you're missing out on investments that would've had a chance to compound interest. As Einstein did once say, "Compound interest is the 8th wonder of the world." You don't want to put this off to the side any longer if you have already.

A different Wealth Snowball approach

Paula attempted to recap JD's strategy but misunderstood his concept. Luckily, she stumbled into an equally interesting approach: The idea is that you save the minimum towards all of your goals, but pour a firehose on one goal until it's completed. Then move on to the next one. This is actually more similar to the debt snowball and a great alternative approach.

If you're saving for a car, a vacation, a house downpayment, *and* your retirement—contribute whatever you deem is the minimum to each goal with each paycheck, but put as much as you can towards one of these, perhaps the easiest to accomplish. In this example, perhaps your vacation fund gets the bulk of that $500 you plan to save.

Which is better?

Any strategy is better than no strategy, but I do like JD's strategy of wealth snowball more than Paula's because JD's focuses exclusively on investing for the long-term and your retirement. Personally, I don't view saving for a vacation or car as savings. That's saving to *spend*. If you want to be advanced, pair JD's wealth snowball concept with a focus on continuing to widen the gap between your earning and your spending and invest the difference. For example, if your savings rate—the amount you save divided by your income—is 15% now, see if you can get it up to 25% by the end of the year (or any 365-day period).

FINAL THOUGHTS AND TAKEAWAYS

The key to building a wealth snowball is three-fold. If I can be dramatic for a moment, what's ahead is life-changing, and all you need to know about money in one sentence:

The steps to building a wealth snowball are to be debt-free, invest your savings as aggressively as you can (especially when you're young), and focus on widening the gap between your income and expenses so you can leverage the power of compound interest.

Start with a small amount invested, invest consistently, and allow your money to grow exponentially. That one sentence alone has the power to unlock your money growth mindset and guide you on your journey to early retirement.

CHAPTER TWELVE

How To Live Rich When You're Not Rich (yet)

It's not all about the money...

Having the right mindset changes everything. Your outlook on your future reflects the actions you're going to take today. As important as your FIRE journey is, your mindset is the precursor to how successful you'll actually be. This section explores the right frame of mind to have to get you on the right path to financial freedom.

During my FIRE journey, I realized there are many ways you can live rich, even if you aren't rich (yet). The first few tips are tactical action strategies that require a certain mindset. Then I'll cover the mental approach to living a more rich, as in fulfilling, life.

Live rich by starting a side hustle or gig that you love

Start that side hustle you've been thinking about, even if it doesn't make money at first. Find something you've always wanted to do. Research it first and ask yourself if you think you can achieve it, even if it's only once. See if you like it, better yet, find the thing that gets you out of bed. You need to have at least one thing that boosts your happiness and helps you feel connected to a greater purpose in life. Then, make time for it as often as you can, knowing that it will help you be a better person and live a financially richer and more fulfilling life

I write a lot about pursuing your purpose. You'll know you found it when the inspiration to do the work comes from within. Plus, if it's congruent with your values, you'll stick with it. You'll be more likely to push through struggles. You won't be driven strictly by results. Not to mention, you'll be diversifying your income in the process.

I started 2021 with a very challenging goal of turning my side hustles into $5,000 of monthly income. Honestly, I rarely think about that goal anymore. That's because I fell in love with the work. Set a goal if that helps you get started. If you are now getting started, think about what you would do even if you weren't paid. Then go for it! If you love it and stick with it, the money will follow.

Build up an F.U. money fund

If you build up a savings run-rate of 12 or more months of expenses, it completely changes how you view your 9 to 5. Most people *need* their job. The company knows this as well. Your employer has leverage and holds power in this situation.

When you're living paycheck to paycheck, you go above and beyond to impress. You show up to work early. You make time for mindless small talk. You never decline a meeting invite. You don't ask for a raise or speak up when you're passed up for a promotion. You're a "yes" man or woman.

On the other hand, when you have a solid cash position, $20,000, $30,000, $50,000 or more that isn't earmarked for anything, you realize you could quit your job at any moment and be fine. Happier even. You could walk away if you feel mistreated. You could even take a mini-retirement (in Part 3 we'll cover a chapter on mini-retirements). You could accept a lower-paying job you actually enjoy. You feel in control, and there's freedom with control. It gives you confidence and courage to say no. Heck, it gives you confidence in general. Don't ever say F.U. to anybody or go all Jerry Maguire on the office, but you'll definitely feel free knowing you could fire your boss.

Outsource your time

I still struggle with this one. However, when I do spend a little money to buy back some time, it feels really, really good. As I'll discuss more in Chapter 13, I revealed at the end of a YouTube video I paid someone on Fiverr to edit the video for $50. He did a great job and saved me 5 or more hours of time. I used that time to work on wedding planning with my then fiancé over beer. That last part is key. If you're going to pay someone for something you could have done to free up your time—be productive or intentional with that time. Work on that side hustle. Get some exercise. Research an investment. Go on a date instead of cleaning your house on a Sunday afternoon. Start that book you've always wanted to write. Or simply enjoy some downtime —get a massage or take your dog to the park.

Either way, buying your time is definitely a rich life habit. The wealthy and successful understand the value of their time and use it to their advantage. They don't waste time doing things that they don't benefit from. It's admittedly less easy to do with little to no money, *but* you don't have to be rich to live rich. It's not a luxury to buy your time. It's an investment. **In life, we first trade our time for money. We then trade our money for time. That's living rich. Most people never consider the latter.**

What's something you could outsource? Give it a shot!

Focus on impressing yourself, not others

I don't dwell on mistakes in the past. I focus on the future. I focus on getting 1% better every day financially and otherwise. With every video I create or book I write, I want to show obvious improvement. I want to impress myself. I want to be happy with the man in the mirror today, tomorrow, and 10 years from now.

I recently listened to Matthew McConaughey's book Green Lights, and it reminded me of what he said during his best actor acceptance speech a few years back. He explained he needs a hero to chase. The twist is he reveals his hero is himself, 10 years in the future. McConaughey says: *"Every day, every week, every month, and every year of my life, my hero is always 10 years away. I'm never gonna be my hero. I'm not gonna attain that. I know I'm not, and that's fine with me because that keeps me with somebody to keep on chasing."*

At first, I was turned off by this. It sounded arrogant to call yourself your hero. It's actually genius. Work hard now to impress your future self—to become the man or woman you want to be.

Future You doesn't care about the toys or gadgets you have or how big your TV or boat is. Future, you doesn't even care how much money you make. Future You cares about how much money you save and invest. Future You cares about how you treat people. Future You cares that you dream big because it's your life—and you only get one. Keep chasing greatness. Future You is watching you and saying *"alright alright alright!"* (I couldn't resist, sorry)

Develop an abundance mindset

Most people think with a scarcity mindset. It's likely you do this at times. I did this for a few negative years in my life. A scarcity mindset is the thought and true belief that there is not enough out there in the world for you—that there will never be enough. Your earning potential is limited. Your savings potential is limited. This results in feeling fear, stress, and anxiety. It really limits us to what's possible and what opportunities are out there. It's a limiting belief that prevents clarity.

An abundance mindset is grounded in the belief that there is more than enough for everyone. It flows out of a deep inner sense of personal worth and security. It helps you develop gratitude and optimism about the world and your money. Abundance is knowing that you can create more wealth in your life. There is enough for you, and it can come from many sources if you put in the work. With the right mindset, you are limitless. Your potential. Your income. Your savings… all *limitless*. Scarcity thinkers say, *why is this happening to me*? Abundance thinkers say, *what more is here for me*? Work on the latter when you catch yourself thinking like the former.

Remind yourself that everything evens out in the wash

Stop obsessing over every shared dollar or expense. A lot of people keep a mental tab in their heads when it comes to their friends and who is supposed to pick up the next bill. Some married couples even put one another on an allowance for the week. This kind of nickel and diming is damaging and the opposite of living free.

My wife and I keep a Google Doc of shared expenses. I made a video about how we do it. Its purpose is to make sure we're in the same ballpark financially. I believe in tracking and keeping it fair to some degree, but I eliminated the decimals on the spreadsheet as a mental reminder to myself that we don't have to be perfect. Nobody does. When we got married, we combined accounts. I couldn't wait for it to all be "our money." We trusted that we're both doing our best financially, and that's all you can ask for. The point is to not get obsessed. It all evens out in the wash in the end.

Keep a long-term focus

Remind yourself that everything works out in the long run, especially if and when you hit a rough patch. Whatever you're going through now, whatever financial stress you feel, know that it will work out eventually. This is a blip—a tiny speed bump in the journey of life. And it's not one you should dwell on. If you think about it, life is really full of changes and challenges. Remind yourself in difficult moments that this too shall pass.

I'm not big on fate, but I know things will work out in the future because, looking back, they always have. Everything is a learning experience. A growing opportunity. This goes back to abundance and positivity. **Positive things happen to positive people.**

As corny as it is, I often remind myself: *Frankie, the last thing you'll be thinking about on your deathbed is 'I should have spent less on groceries.' 'Why did I pay full price for the rug?' 'I could have gotten a better interest rate if I had only shopped around.'*

Do your best. That's all you can do. You won't be perfect, but appreciate what you have. Live rich and free, mentally.

FINAL THOUGHTS AND TAKEAWAYS

Those are my top strategic tips and mindset shifts to help you live a more rich life, with or without money. A person's happiness in life isn't measured by checking to-do boxes, zeros in a bank account, or material objects. The richest lives are lived by those who care less about money and more about the future, relationships, and personal growth.

The moment I stopped fixating on monthly income goals and focused instead on pursuing my passions in life, expressing creativity, buying back my time, spending money without guilt, and forming strong relationships, I started living a more rich life. I started really *living*. Rich goes well beyond financial best practices. It is a series of learned lessons reflected on. It's getting 1% better daily. It's about making good decisions day in and day out. It's living without regret.

Becoming rich has its best practices financially, but living rich is about developing a positive money mindset. It's not resting on your laurels. It's expressing gratitude often. It's being kind to yourself and one another. And it's doing your best. If you can honestly say that you're proud of the way you are living your life at this moment, I have no doubt that a rich and happy life will find you if it hasn't already. And by rich, now you know I don't mean wealthy.

CHAPTER THIRTEEN

The Paradox of Wealth

Time isn't money. Money is time.

Fictional character Howard Stark once said, "No amount of money ever bought a second of time." I completely disagree with that statement. Understanding the paradox of wealth will help you achieve true financial freedom. It'll help you understand the entire point of money and how to actually win the game of wealth.

Time and money

There is a mindset shift required when it comes to how we think about time and money. Until we understand the wealth paradox and change our behavior accordingly, we will never create the wealth and lifestyle we're looking for. Otherwise, you might end up monetarily rich but time-poor.

Most of us have a friend or relative that always says "busy" as a reply to the question: *How have you been?* Anecdotally I've observed the higher the income of the person, the more likely they are to respond that way. The paradox has to do with the relationship between time and money. The point of money, as a tool, is to buy back your time. And I absolutely mean this literally.

Perspective

As you earn more, money changes how you see the world and look at things. It has for me. By no means do I have a lot of it, but as I grow my net worth and create more income streams, it's opening up my eyes to this idea. I'm finding that the more things I can afford to buy, the fewer things I want to own. I've realized I don't need things to be happy. I need experience. In order to have more of those, I need time.

If you buy time instead of things, you can have more experiences and live a more rich life. That's a key ingredient to unlocking financial freedom and early retirement.

Phases of wealth

There are two phases of wealth in life, and the second is overlooked by many. First, you exchange your time for money. This is the wealth-gathering phase. But, eventually, the goal is (or should be) to exchange your money for time. This part is critical. If you constantly exchange most or all of your money for things, you won't have any money left over to buy time.

Buying time could certainly be grand and symbolic, like walking away from a job you don't enjoy or taking a mini-retirement to avoid burnout. But it might not be that extreme.

Take some time and think about this: if you had the money, what thing or things would you rather outsource to give you time back? If you're a business owner, this is an essential exercise no matter how much money you currently have, profitable or not.

I'd spend more quality time with my wife, my family, and dog. I'd read for pleasure more often. I'd travel more. I'd plan a spontaneous weekend camping road trip. At the very least, I'd definitely avoid burnout by finding balance. And I'd certainly have more time to just think—to discover more clarity.

Thought exercise

Here is an exercise to help you find more clarity regarding time and money. Get out a piece of paper and make two columns. On the left: list ways you could get more of your time back—even if it cost you money. Think really creatively. On the right: list what you would do with this newfound time. What would you prioritize in life? Aim for 10 ideas in each column.

Tip: More than likely, the things that come to mind first are likely your top priorities.

You're already doing it

If this idea of buying your time back sounds crazy, consider this: most of you are already doing it on some level. For example:

- Eating at a restaurant or ordering takeout instead of cooking at home and doing dishes.
- Getting your car's oil changed instead of doing it yourself.
- Taking an Uber instead of driving, biking, or bussing to work.
- Paying retail price instead of looking for a good deal.
- Paying someone to mow your lawn.
- Paying a plumber rather than getting a few parts at Home Depot and figuring it out yourself.

If only you could pay someone to exercise for you…

You can't, but you can hire a personal trainer to keep you motivated! They can be expensive but very worth it. It forces you to show up, which is half the battle, and a professional can help you achieve your goals even faster, saving you time. Plus, improving your physical health means you'll likely have fewer medical expenses in the long run. The best part of all? You're more likely to live longer which again, means you're buying your time back in the most literal sense of all.

Failure to plan

Once you have more money than time, I hope you shift the way you view life and make decisions, no matter how big or small. Almost every time-sucking problem is solvable with a little research and a little money. Many entrepreneurs and high earners fail to recognize the effectiveness of buying back time without realizing it. Many say they value time over money, but their work calendars and personal schedules tell a different story. They rarely look at the day or week ahead and proactively think about how to get more time back, even if it means spending a little bit of money.

For example, entrepreneurs and business owners could:

- Find a bookkeeper.
- Say no to low-priority meetings or block off time for "heads-down" work.
- Hire a property manager to manage your rental properties.
- Pay someone to run more effective ads.
- Add headcount and hire well in general.

Buying back time happens in big meaningful ways. Building a business or buying investments that pay you, no matter how much time you spend working on them, is big and meaningful. When you build assets or buy them, you start to remove yourself from trading your time for money.

Many people think to build wealth; you need to put in extra time. It's very easy to fall back into doing things yourself or thinking you're the only one that can do the job right. And I get it.

Letting go

I haven't let go. I'm still a one-man show on YouTube. My channel is my baby. My world. But getting help is inevitable, and I have done it in the past. In writing 2 previous books, I hired 4 people on the creation side. I "hired" 6 friends on the beta reader feedback side. I spent hundreds, if not thousands, just to get those books produced. But I still have a mental hurdle I can't get over when it comes to YouTube. What I need to internalize, and maybe you do too, is to mentally separate the short-term spending from the long-term benefits. I'll come back to an experiment I ran to help with this in a moment.

Leverage to build wealth

Here's a spin on this wealth paradox: If you're at the beginning of your wealth accumulation phase in your financial journey, you can use The Wealth Paradox to your advantage to make money. First, trade your time for money. You can do small tasks and chores and accept other people's money in exchange for their time back. For example, post some of your skills on sites like Fiverr or Upwork. As you grow your wealth, increase your savings rate, buy investments, and develop a "money is time" mentality.

Do less

The paradox of wealth is to do *less*. It's to buy back time in a literal sense and to use that extra time to enjoy life more. People think the endgame of wealth is to acquire as much money as possible. If that's the case, you'll never cross a finish line or internalize the satisfaction of doing so. Acquiring wealth only gets you halfway there.

The goal of money is to accumulate enough so you can stop trading your time for money. It's to trade your money for time. With time back you are free to pursue a passion. Spend more time with loved ones. Slow down and appreciate everything. Stop and actually smell the roses. Do things you didn't know were possible. You're able to live fully.

I like to think of wealth as a way to become a time investor. Buy assets, things, and services that give you time back because time is the best asset you can buy—your most valuable resource. Ultimately, it's the only non-renewable resource that we have. You have to design your life to free up your time because none of us know how much of it is left. It's the most precious commodity of all. Cherish it. Prioritize it consciously and constantly.

Two takeaways

#1. As a thought exercise, think about and write down: What could you spend money on or do to get more time back? Then, what would you do with that newfound time?

#2. Action on the idea of giving yourself permission to spend money on help, resources, or anything that gives you time back.

It's a big idea and a total mindset shift but starts on a small scale as practice. Here are some quick, practical ideas:

- Pay to get your groceries delivered or meal prep.
- Hire a virtual assistant to tackle your "busy work."
- Put your kids on an hourly rate for a week and see what chores they can accomplish that you typically do.
- Hire a babysitter.
- Pay to learn a skill so you can do something more quickly and efficiently.
- Take an online course to master your finances (Save Money Resolution is great and 90% off with code SAVEHALFBOOK - shameless plug, sorry!).

The ideas are endless personally and professionally.

When you start to do this on a small scale, it'll help you step back and think about the big picture. It'll help you enjoy life and work more. It'll help you appreciate what you have that aren't things. It'll give you time to just relax—to find some peace in this noisy world. To find clarity and focus. To internalize what extra time looks like in early retirement.

This paradox of wealth is all about finding balance and alignment between time and money. **Exchange your time for money. Then exchange your money for time.** Spending time reflecting on this idea might be the motivation you need to get good with money, to learn more about the FIRE Movement and early retirement, or to think critically about your why of money, your why of work, and your why of life and living.

A personal experiment

As an experiment, I paid someone on Fiverr to edit the video companion for this chapter. It likely saved me 6 or 7 hours of work. It cost me $50. Is that worth it? It's very unlikely I'll get an instant return on outsourcing editing. But, if I do it enough, find the right people, and continue to learn how to outsource effectively, I can focus on what I do best: research, write, and create more valuable content.

What's one thing you should be outsourcing that you aren't outsourcing yet? How could you buy back your time? Spend time reflecting on this if you haven't. When you have and you're ready, let's put on our walking shoes and help you find your exact FIRE path. We'll learn how to walk. Then we'll learn how to run!

Don't forget: *There's a companion video for EVERY chapter in this book listed in References at the end! You can also find them all via the "Save Half, Retire Fast" playlist on The Money Resolution channel. It's perfect for visual learners like me!*

Part III

Types of FIRE

CHAPTER FOURTEEN

Fat FIRE vs Lean FIRE

Choose Your Own Financial Freedom Adventure

How much do you want to be able to spend in retirement? That's the ultimate question for anyone considering FIRE. In the chapters that follow, I will detail the 10 most common FIRE strategies, beginning with Traditional FIRE and two extremes.

There are infinite paths to pursuing FIRE and I find this to be the refreshing part of the FIRE Movement that really opened up my eyes. Ideally one or two speaks to you most. Let's start by reviewing the most known and most commonly followed path:

Traditional FIRE

Traditional FIRE starts by finding your FIRE number, which is the exact amount of money you need saved and invested to conceivably never run out of money during extended retirement. That's because the bulk of your money stays invested during retirement, so it continues to compound and grow.

The formula is to determine your expected annual expenses in retirement, then multiply it by 25. You want to make sure you're accounting for inflation. If you project your expenses will be $50,000 a year, you'll need $1,250,000 saved and invested. Then, each year you'll live off of 4% of your total portfolio if you want to leverage the 4% rule. Ideally, you pull out dividends, so your investment remains invested. You'll want to do this wisely to avoid paying extra taxes or any taxes for that matter. You also want to avoid any fees for tapping retirement accounts early.

Again, Traditional FIRE is achieved at 25 times your expected annual expenses. At that point, work becomes fully optional. In this situation, studies show you're very unlikely to run out of money with a reasonable degree of certainty.

Let's continue the many FIRE paths discussion by comparing 2 very different sides of the financial independence movement: Fat FIRE and Lean FIRE.

Fat FIRE

The "fat" in Fat FIRE alludes to the idea that you'll have "fat" pockets of money in early retirement. Fat FIRE allows you to live off an upper-middle-class income in retirement. Your Fat FIRE number will vary depending on location and desired lifestyle, but a common number is annual spending of $100,000 a year in retirement. This means you'd need to have no less than $2.5 million invested based on the 4% rule to be financially independent.

With Fat FIRE, it will take you longer to reach financial independence but allows you to live off of a pretty healthy income in retirement. Spending $100,000 or more a year in retirement may sound like a lot but, due to inflation, the cost of living could be considerably higher 20 to 30 years from now. Maybe $100,000 a year isn't so crazy after all. If nothing else, at least it sounds fun to not work *and* spend $100,000+ a year, right?

If you're not sure how to come up with a Fat FIRE number to strive for, here's one way: Think about your highest spending year of the last 10 years as a starting point. Then consider going about 20% higher than that. Then, 25x *that* number. I'm simplifying, and it's not simple to predict your future spending, but this should give you one exercise to consider as a starting point for a goal.

Fat FIRE Pros and Cons

One of the biggest advantages of Fat FIRE is you have a large cushion to work with. You'll be more prepared for the unexpected. Plus, because you *can* spend $100,000 a year in retirement doesn't mean you *will*. Perhaps you spend between $70,000-$80,000 and hold onto the rest in case of emergency, a health emergency for example.

Fat FIRE means more freedom, flexibility, and protection from emergencies and the unknown. I'm sure you can see why it's appealing to many. However, actually saving and investing $2.5 million can be a completely different story so the pros and cons are relatively obvious:

Pros

- The safety in having more money saved and invested.
- You can live a more lavish lifestyle like traveling often if desired.

Cons

- It can be very difficult to save and invest a nest egg of $2.5–5M. That's very difficult on any budget and it's near impossible for lower-income earners. Whereas, traditional FIRE and especially Lean FI are accessible to anybody with the right mindset, education, and approach to everyday life.

Lean FIRE

According to The Fioneers website: "Lean FIRE is when someone has saved up 25 times their annual expenses and lives on a 'lean' budget, spending less than the average American (which is around $60,000 a year)."

With Lean FIRE, many plan to live off of $40,000 a year or even less in retirement. That means saving and investing $1 million or maybe as *little* as $750,000 if you can live off of only $30,000 a year in retirement. The big question becomes: can you live off of $30,000 to $40,000 a year in retirement? It's not quite the opposite of Fat FIRE (because the opposite would be a zero-dollar net worth, am I right?). Both of these mean working hard to save and invest money aggressively. However, the difference lies in the final number investment goal.

One consideration to keep in mind when evaluating Lean FIRE is, most people don't realize that your expenses can (and conceivable should) come down later in life. For example, a good majority of people will have paid off their mortgage or will be close to paying off their mortgage come retirement. In other words, they may not need to pay for housing. Plus, since you're not working 260 days of the year, your transportation costs might naturally become much lower.

Additionally, when you're on the other side of 50 or 60, you may not have a strong desire, or the health, to travel far and often for fun. For many, home and family is where the heart is in older age. By then you might have grandkids you want to spend time with, keeping you pretty grounded.

But what about the unexpected? After all, health care costs can and likely will be your biggest cost come retirement in older age. At that point, nothing is guaranteed. Especially your health. That's the reality.

Pro Tip: Max out your HSAs annually in your working years. If you have access to one but don't have one, get one! You can contribute $3,600 annually as of 2021 and these can offer triple-tax benefits. HSA's are tax-free contributions, tax-free growth, and withdrawals are tax-free.

Pros

- It takes far less time to reach financial independence—it's quicker than Regular FIRE and much quicker to reach than Fat FIRE. Save aggressively now, live off less later in life.
- The major pro is that work becomes optional much sooner.

Cons

- You'll have less money available to deal with unexpected emergencies or long-term care.
- You'll live a much more humble life of course.

Regardless, don't be in a hurry. You can't force the early

retirement issue. Instead, enjoy the journey, it's the best part. I would argue it's even better than the end destination. As much as I want to be retired, I don't necessarily want to be older. That sounds strange but I imagine that's true for most.

FINAL THOUGHTS AND TAKEAWAYS

Based on what I've learned and my goals, I stand somewhere in the middle. I've gotten my annual expenses down to around $50,000 a year despite living in a big city. I don't know how much I'll earn and save when I hopefully take the leap to work for myself full time. I have a strong itch to travel more—maybe 2 to 3 times a year, especially in retirement. I don't have kids but I want to have them. In other words, I'm young with a lot of unknowns ahead.

My personal thoughts and situation are all over the place. That's normal! That's probably you too. There's so much to consider and so much unknown ahead for all of us. However, what I do know is that I sleep 10 times better knowing about FIRE and the 4% rule and knowing there are *lots* of different FIRE paths. I don't have to pick a lane and obsessively strive for it. I need to be consistent. *I need to keep learning, keep going, and take it one day at a time.*

Everything you learn is a tool in your toolbag. Knowing there are so many options to reaching FI can be encouraging and motivating. I've only covered 2 beyond Traditional FIRE so far and your path likely isn't linear. Maybe you love the idea of Lean FI, especially if you're now getting started. It's an accessible way to get on the path towards financial freedom and retiring early. Then, once you reduce your expenses and increase your savings rate you might find standard FIRE more appealing. You get the idea: Start Lean. Move to Standard. And who knows, you might consider Fat FI eventually.

Knowing the lanes gets you on the track and positioned to stay on track. It's excellent to pick a lane and chase after it, but don't get fixed in your ways. Have a plan. Get after it, but be flexible. Roll with the punches. Keep learning. Keep earning. Enjoy the ride. If you want to slow down to enjoy the ride, these next two FIRE types might be for you.

CHAPTER FIFTEEN

Slow FIRE vs Coast FIRE

No Path is Linear

If you are the type of person who's not in a hurry to retire as fast as possible, there are two types of FIRE that you might consider taking a closer look at. Slow FIRE and Coast FIRE are for those who want to have financial freedom, but take a different, more balanced approach in meeting their goals. Both have their similarities, but also have their key differences.

Slow FIRE

Slow financial independence aims to strike a balance between enjoying the process as much as the destination. If you're on the Slow FIRE path, you're not in a rush. You care most about being happy and fiscally responsible at the same time. Balance and happiness are key. It's about living in the moment while creating a simple plan to automate your way to financial independence.

It may be as simple as maxing out a 401(k) each year, but little else in terms of saving or investing. Those pursuing Slow FIRE aren't in a hurry to get to the retirement finish line—which I've explained is commonly recognized as 25 times your annual expenses. Instead, they get on the path, do 1 or 2 things really right, and otherwise slow down and enjoy life.

That's because Slow Financial Independence is *not* about achieving early retirement as quickly as possible. Despite traditional and even extreme FIRE stories we've heard about (people retiring in their early 30's), slow FIRE is an excellent alternative lifestyle. Slow and steady still wins the race.

On the blog The Fioneers, they explained: "Our journey focuses on discovering our values, envisioning our ideal lives, and aligning our daily lives with that vision along the way." The goal is still to reach complete financial independence, but there's no specific timeframe or target date for the most part. "It's when someone utilizes the incremental financial freedom they gain along the journey to financial independence to live happier and healthier lives, do better work, and build strong relationships."

Someone pursuing Slow FIRE may still enjoy traveling, taking 1 or 2 vacations a year, or decide to leave a higher-paying job for a lower-paying one if that means being happier. Many will also go above and beyond their standard 9 to 5 with a second job or side hustle. This may sound very familiar to Lean FIRE. Lean FIRE is living on $40,000 or less in retirement, so your ultimate retirement number is lower than most. The difference is that it can and probably will take more time to achieve Slow FIRE than Lean FIRE.

Pros

- You'll likely enjoy the journey along the way a bit more, because YOLO-BBS (you only live once, but be smart).
- It doesn't take a lot of detailed thought and effort.

Cons

- It takes much longer to reach your final destination.
- You will be much older when you reap what you sowed.

Coast FIRE

Similar to Slow FIRE, Coast FIRE rejects the idea that you should try to reach financial independence as soon as possible. However, there are a lot of differences with these I'll try to pull apart. With Coast FIRE, it means spending the next handful of years saving as aggressively as you can. Then you pull your foot off the gas pedal for the rest of your working career while your early investments grow and have a better opportunity to compound.

It's saving up enough at a very young age that you can stop contributing to savings and investments. Then your money continues to grow via compound interest. All you need to know is how much annual income you want to live off of come retirement to officially retire. With Coast FIRE, you save to a target number by a certain age and then stop saving and let compounding gains "coast" you to your ultimate target retirement nest egg. You get relatively close to your financial independence number, then you can quit your main job and instead take on a part-time job and/or build passive income streams to live off of to cover life's basic expenses. Then you simply wait for your portfolio to grow large enough to hit your official FIRE number.

In other words, you go hot out of the gate with aggressive saving and investing. Then, say no thanks to a full-time no-fun desk job. Instead, you do what you want for some income to live off of. With Slow FIRE, you do one or two things really right, like max out your 401(k) and/or a Roth IRA annually. With Coast FIRE, you save half or potentially a lot more than that for a handful of years so you can jump-start your investments and take full advantage of compound interest.

As you can imagine, It may be difficult to achieve Coast FIRE unless you start early. Otherwise, you might be waiting at that part-time job longer than you expected because compound interest isn't working as much in your favor as it would be otherwise.

This brings up an interesting question about timelines. You might be wondering when you can start coasting. I've seen it commonly suggested to do it 5 years before reaching your expected 25x your expenses number. Although, according to the calculators, it may be as long as 10 or 15 years early. It's unique for everyone.

The Calculation

Speaking of calculators, let's briefly discuss numbers. Below is the official calculation. If this makes sense to you, great. Stop here and jot it down and work through it.

Coast FI = FI # / (1+expected growth rate) ^ # of years to retirement

Example: $750{,}000 / (1+.05)^{22}$

For the rest of us, there's an easier way. It's an online Coast FI calculator, of course! I recommend one from WalletBurst. Let's walk through an example. It's very similar to most retirement calculators, but this one helps you see when you can coast.

We'll use round numbers starting at age 30. This person (we'll call him Joe) wants to achieve Coast FIRE starting at age 50. He plans to spend $50,000 in retirement. He currently has $50,000 saved. He contributes $2,500 a month. Yes, that's relatively aggressive, but you'll need to be. His stretch goal is to coast at age 45, but he won't make it unless inflation is 2.5% and his rate of growth is 13%, which is very unlikely. I wouldn't recommend any estimations over 10% earned on investments. I prefer to project either 7% or 8% to be more realistic. So, at 8%, with inflation set at 2.5% a year, Joe could coast at age 50 with his approach. Try out the calculator if you're curious to find your Coast FI number.

The big idea is: Why sprint to the finish line if you can coast? Slow down and enjoy life more than you have before. Work less and do something you enjoy instead.

With Traditional FIRE, you sprint the whole time and get there quicker. However, when you get to the finish line, you might find yourself feeling really… bored. Some people simply don't know what to do with themselves when they "work themselves to death", then suddenly have all the free time in the world. With all this extra free time, it can lead to thoughts of feeling purposeless or lost. It's like having your bags packed, but nowhere to go.

With Coast FIRE, taking on a part-time job or building up passive income streams gives you something to do that may lead to a hobby in retirement—or at least prevent the shock of going from 100 MPH to zero.

Paraphrasing the blog FIRE The Family, one reason to take on a part-time job while coasting is for the benefits. They list these 10 companies that offer benefits to part-time employees: *Lowes, REI,*

Staples, Starbucks, UPS, USPS, Whole Foods Market, Home Depot, Costco, Walmart.

You could take on a part-time job with benefits like one of these, *or* you could quit your job to take a lower-paying one that you are more passionate about. You could freelance or run your own business. You could get a seasonal job, *or* one partner may be able to quit completely. You could also turn down a promotion that would ultimately stress you out.

Pros

- You can work less earlier in life than you would with Traditional FIRE.
- You might discover a hobby or passion via part-time work.

Cons

- You won't be able to fully quit the workforce as soon as Traditional FIRE.
- The math can get a little complicated.

FINAL THOUGHTS AND TAKEAWAYS

Anecdotally, Coast FIRE appears to be on track to rival Traditional FIRE in terms of popularity but Slow FIRE certainly has a solid contingency of followers. Both put an emphasis on balance during the journey at some point. Balance is key and both offer this as a pro. But if you're looking for something else, something a little more unique to you and yours, I still have 5 types of FIRE I'll cover relatively quickly.

CHAPTER SIXTEEN

5 More Types of FIRE

There's a FIRE For Everyone

This chapter is dedicated to a summary of other common types of FIRE that you can choose from that could best align with your mindset, values, and goals. Each FIRE type is about getting better with your money so you can live a more rich and free life with more options. Everyone can benefit from the principles of FIRE because planning for the future, intentional spending, and good investing strategies are valuable lessons to internalize whether you want to retire early or not.

It's a misconception that achieving FIRE means quitting work forever. Again, it's about having the option to work or not. As you'll see, with several of these types of FIRE, work is still involved to some degree for many. Either way, financial independence is not a race, as there are many paths to becoming financially independent quickly and slowly.

Obese FIRE

Obese FIRE is planning to retire with $5 to $10 million in the bank —or rather invested. You likely need to be a very high earner, or you're not starting from scratch. Perhaps some of your wealth was inherited, and you're used to an elevated lifestyle.

FIRE can absolutely mean wanting more, and you see that with

Obese FIRE. Maybe you only retire 5 or 10 years early, but when you do, YOLO is the name of the game. Who says the last 20, 30, or 40 years of your life can't be your best lived? On the other hand, someone seeking Obese FIRE might want to create and hand down generational wealth. They want to leave a legacy. They want to help future generations and encourage them to pay it forward as well. Plus, you know what they say: *Aim for the Obese FIRE stars, land amongst the Fat FIRE moon.* Or something like that...

Barista FIRE

AKA Burger Flipper FIRE. Barista FIRE is having saved enough to retire early but choosing to work part-time, mainly for health insurance and other benefits. Starbucks is an example of a place you can work with good benefits.

You have enough invested to retire from your main job early. But, instead of not working at all, people may use their financial independence to work part-time, do freelance work, or pursue a dream career that is less well-paid. It gives you the choice of working for pleasure rather than working to live.

You are withdrawing money from your portfolio but then supplementing it with that part-time income, a bit similar to Coast FIRE. Instead of the corporate work environment, you can work at a coffee shop, take part in the gig economy, or work somewhere for limited hours a week. This is also an option for those who maybe aren't sure about early retirement and want to test it out a bit. Plus, it lets you explore more of your passions, side hustles or helps you find something you might love to do for full-time work. Ideally, the job includes benefits.

Flamingo FIRE

The name comes from the Money Flamingo blog, which is great! Flamingo FIRE is a combination of 3 types of retirement lifestyles: semi-retirement, early retirement, and traditional retirement. There are 3 phases:

First is the accumulation phase, where you work full time and build up a nest egg, saving and investing as much as possible. When you've reached half of your FIRE number, you enter phase 2: Semi-retirement. Your nest egg will keep growing while you work, but you only work to cover your living expenses. If you earn 7% on those investments, you can use the Rule of 72 to know your money is going to double in roughly 10 years.

During those 10 years, you don't have to add to your nest egg at all. As long as it doubles in 10 years, you're ready to retire. Until then, you can work part-time or work a different job that makes you happy, even if it doesn't pay as well. Once you hit 25 times your expected living expenses, you've reached full FIRE, which is stage 3.

Baby FIRE

This one is similar to Coast & Barista FIRE in that you still likely work part-time to cover some of your expenses but add in a literal baby. The aim is to save and invest enough to cover your expenses during extended maternity leave so that either one or both parents can have a significant amount of time off of work while the child or children are young.

For example, if the mother of the child works part-time and brings in $12,000 a year, a fifth of the couple's $60,000 a year in projected expenses, the partner would need to earn $48,000 per year to cover the remaining expenses. That still may not require full-time work. Ideally, both parents can extend time off or work part-time, so they can spend precious time with their new family. Alternatively, couples can save and invest as much as they can for a couple of years right after marriage until a baby arrives. Then they both take a year off from work, for example. Some call saving aggressively to take a year off a "mini-retirement."

Hybrid FIRE

AKA Choose Your Own Adventure FIRE. Admittedly I made this up, but it brings me to a really important point. There is no singular path to financial independence and early retirement. Even if you pick a path and go all in, life can and will get in the way. Plans get derailed. Emergencies happen because life happens.

Be prepared to be flexible. The one thing you can surely expect in life is the unexpected. They say the only surprise in a day is a day without surprises. Don't get discouraged if you get off track. Don't hesitate to take a hybrid approach and combine 2 or 3 of the FIRE paths I've covered. In fact, many people have commented on my YouTube FIRE videos that they are taking a hybrid approach of X + Y and sometimes Z. If that's you, that's great!

FINAL THOUGHTS AND TAKEAWAYS

I'll leave you with this question and reminder to ponder, if you haven't already: What's your why of FI? Always remember, your why is far more important than the tactical how. If it's simply because you want to quit your job and escape your 9 to 5, you're likely doing it wrong. FIRE should never be about running from something. It should be about running *to* something. And always remember, the path isn't linear. Choose one approach. Combine concepts from several. Change your mind. Flexibility and consistency are what matter most.

We've covered 10 types of FIRE but let's take a step back and take a more critical look at the difference between financial independence and financial freedom.

CHAPTER SEVENTEEN

Financial Independence vs. Financial Freedom

This key difference changes everything...

Financial independence and financial freedom. There are plenty of definitions and ways to think about these terms. In fact, they are often used interchangeably in the personal finance space. However, by framing them as two distinct ideas, with financial independence as a numerical goal and financial freedom as a state of mind, you will ultimately lead a more meaningful and successful financial journey.

While financial independence is an amazing goal, achieving a mindset of financial freedom is equally important. It is also possible to reach financial freedom and the benefits that come with it, well before you reach financial independence.

What is financial independence?

As a general definition, you reach financial independence when you have enough assets, investments, and passive income to cover your expenses. If you maintain the same lifestyle, you can reasonably expect to never run out of money without *needing* to work. When you are financially independent, you choose how you want to spend your time. You can pursue your passions, travel, or volunteer. You name it!

Though there are different equations for determining when you have reached financial independence, it is typically a mathematical calculation: 25 times your annual expenses. It is achieved when you reach a certain net worth. For most people, this is a massive goal. It may mean saving up a million dollars or more. This could be years or decades away.

What is financial freedom?

Financial freedom is not a number. It is a mindset. It is when money no longer drives your decisions. You are guided by your passions and values as opposed to price. One way to illustrate this concept is through three levels of wealth or three ways that people tend to think about their money and how to spend it:

1. **Price:** The exact dollar amount. You only care about how much you are spending.
2. **Cost**: The overall economic impact. You consider what you are getting for the price.
3. **Value**: Your personal feeling of satisfaction. Does this item or experience align with your core values? Does it bring you happiness?

As you move up these levels, you start to take on more of an investor mindset. You reach financial freedom when you think in terms of value first, cost second, and price third. Financial freedom is when money is no longer the primary reason that you do or don't do something. Price alone does not determine your actions.

What would your life look like if you were financially free?

Another way to understand financial freedom is to think about what currently stresses you out about money. What could change if you were at peace with your finances? For one person, reaching financial freedom is when they are completely out of debt. For another, it is when they can go to the grocery store and have absolute confidence that they have enough money in their account to cover the bill. For you, it could mean having enough saved up to quit a job that is making you miserable.

The key is that being financially free is not achieving a certain net worth. It is different for everyone because it is a state of mind. It is no longer feeling a constant hum of stress and anxiety about money. It is psychological freedom and financial confidence.

The danger of single-mindedly pursuing financial independence

If you pursue financial independence as a numerical goal, without analyzing what you need to feel financially *free*, the journey will be more difficult and unpleasant. Even when you have reached a point where you could make decisions to greatly improve your life, you may continue taking actions that make you unhappy because all you care about is reaching financial independence as quickly as possible.

For example, you may choose to keep working long hours or sacrificing quality time with your family. You may turn down a job that you are passionate about simply because the salary is less than ideal. Even though money is not scarce, you still make decisions with a scarcity mindset.

Financial independence as a goal is simply a number. However, it's possible that when you achieve it, you still may not be happy. Financial freedom, on the other hand, means starting to live the life that you want to live, and it is achievable well before you reach financial independence. Even with less money, you may discover more happiness.

You can live a rich life without being rich

Many people may think all they need to do is reach financial independence and be happy. While financial independence is still an incredibly empowering goal for your money, financial freedom is critical for your happiness. Financial freedom means:

- Stressing less about money
- Discovering what you value and what makes you happy
- Being able to spend your money and time in alignment with your values

Once you are financially free, you can make choices that make you happy, even if you are still years away from the mathematical version of financial independence. Once you are financially free, you can make the most out of your life immediately.

CHAPTER EIGHTEEN

A Twist On The FIRE Movement Acronym

This is what FIRE could stand for...

The FIRE acronym stands for financial independence, retire early. I discovered a unique FIRE acronym that was more appealing. I like it because it is more prescriptive than the standard acronym. Financial independence, retire early, describes the desired end result. However, it doesn't explain *how* to get there for beginners.

I was listening to Paula Pant's Afford Anything podcast, and she had the hosts of the Choose FI podcast on as guests. The whole episode was great, and you should give it a listen. It's a deep discussion about the economy and the future of work.

There was one part of the podcast that particularly piqued my interest. Paula shared her framework by saying, "The framework that I like to use is F-I-R-E: F, financial basics. I nail that down first. Then, once the F is taken care of I-R-E: investing, real estate, entrepreneurship. The IRE of FIRE, which all got built on top of financial basics. Take care of the F first, then pivot to focusing on the IRE of FIRE."

I'll cover each part of her unique FIRE definition:

F stands for Financial basics

Start there. Pay off the credit cards. Save up an emergency fund. Establish good credit. Get to net worth positive. She calls this financial solvency, which means having more assets than liabilities. Even knowing the difference between assets and liabilities is key here. As I've mentioned, I wrote a book about mastering financial basics called The Money Resolution. It comes packed with 101 money tips. Find it on Amazon.

That's "F" but Paula believes the IRE in FIRE is the most important part...

I stands for Investing

It's critical you learn and master investing and develop your own strategy and philosophy around it. It's extremely important to start as soon as possible so you can maximize your compound interest growth opportunity.

My strategy is dollar-cost averaging and automation, investing in low-fee index funds that track the entire stock market or S&P 500, and it's prioritizing and maxing out all of my available tax-advantaged retirement accounts before any individual investing. I use M1 Finance for my Roth IRA and rollover 401(k)s from the past and definitely recommend M1 Finance for automation and no-fee trading.

Investing can certainly sound scary at first. I totally get it. It was for me, but scary doesn't mean hard. Like with most things, once you start, it's not as difficult as it sounds. The hardest step is the first, but keep it simple in the beginning and commit to learning. Future You will thank you.

R stands for Real estate

Paula built up $43,000 a year in net rental income by age 34 from 8 rental properties. She became a millionaire before age 30. This is not the norm, and I hesitate to share this because it can be discouraging, especially if you're not as young as her and are still a renter like me. Remember: comparison is the root of unhappiness. Instead, I encourage you to strongly consider real estate ownership as part of your future plans if you're also a renter. It doesn't have to be 8 rental properties. Or even 3. Real estate can be your own home and only that.

My wife and I spent 6 months attempting to buy our first home. We lost out on multiple offers we placed. But a year ago, before learning about homeownership, I was starting to convince myself we should rent forever. I've come around and feel it would be a mistake to rent forever. We may not buy in the next few months or even for years, but after my learning and research, I do think it's wise to buy. (Life update: we purchased my first home in November of 2021!)

Measure twice, cut once when it comes to real estate. Don't rush in due to peer pressure, but learn real estate and consider it for your home and possibly for rental property. It might be your ticket to financial independence like it was for Paula Pant.

E stands for Entrepreneurship

Paula didn't talk about this much in the podcast episode, but it shouldn't be too hard to speculate about her thoughts on entrepreneurship based on what I know about her. Entrepreneurship doesn't necessarily mean starting your own business or coming up with an amazing business idea now from scratch. It could simply mean diversifying your own income.

Side hustle. Learn about passive income. Start a small brand or business online and commit to it for the long term, even if it doesn't make you money at first. When friends and family ask about making money on YouTube I explain *it will take 2 years to make money on YouTube if you make one video a week consistently. But the money you make from something you work hard to build over time is even more satisfying than a desk job paycheck. Plus, it's extra security.*

Learn about and create your own LLC. Learn about tax breaks and benefits. Help people solve a problem as your #1 goal, and you will find success. Aim to be great at whatever you choose to do. In the long run, the cream always rises to the top. Diversify your income and help others in the process. You won't regret it.

The IRE in FIRE

In Paula's version of FIRE, the F was financial basics, but it's the

IRE part of FIRE that really matters. In her words, IRE gives you multiple exit points, as in, exit from your day-to-day 9-to-5 main gig if you do IRE right. The IRE of FIRE leads to true financial independence. If and when you add Paula's version of IRE to the F (financial basics) you'll surely discover financial freedom in time. It's not easy to master investing, real estate, and entrepreneurship, but if you hadn't considered one or some of those, it would be wise to consider those endeavors in your financial journey.

Paula's financial independence explained

Paula Pant explained her definition of financial independence in a few different ways, and they're all very wise. I combined a few of Paula Pant's definitions of financial independence into this clear explanation:

Financial independence is the state in which your passive income, typically through investments, gives you enough of a safety net that you can live fearlessly. It's when you can make decisions from a place of hope and desire, rather than fear or obligation. When most people hear "typically through investments," they think of traditional investing. But investing can also be investing in real estate (whether it's your own home or rental properties), investing in a business, or creating passive income.

Paula's twist on the FIRE acronym is a great reminder that financial independence has many definitions and early retirement has many paths. To each their own when it comes to financial success, but I hope you are encouraged to keep going. Keep pushing. Stay encouraged no matter where you are on your financial journey. Always be learning. Enjoy the ride, and don't get overwhelmed.

Speaking of overwhelm... FIRE isn't all rainbows and lollipops. It's time we confirm the struggles FIRE present from outsider judgment to misconceptions to myths to drawbacks.

Part IV

The Darker Side of FIRE

CHAPTER NINETEEN
Is the FIRE Movement a Cult?

The answer might surprise you

FIRE is clearly a movement. But is it a cult? Some think it's extreme. Are they right? Or is there something more to it? Is it more useful and approachable than most people think?

Inherent bias is hard to set aside completely, but I hope you'll appreciate my mostly objective analytical approach to this question. Let's start by discussing what a cult actually is.

Cults explained

When cults make the news, it almost always falls into the "bad news" category. You hear about the violence. You see the harmful nature of them—especially in documentaries on Netflix. You might hear of the FBI or ATF breaking up cults and that's because cults typically promote illegal behavior within them. As I analyze the FIRE movement through the lens of a cult, it's important we understand the traits a cult possesses and what makes them different from a movement.

A movement in its simplest form is any social group defined by its unique religious, spiritual, or philosophical beliefs. With that definition, political affiliation, religion, and even some hobbies have been called movements. A formal definition of a movement is a series of organized activities working toward an objective or an organized effort to promote or attain an end. That sounds about right for FIRE. But the difference between a movement and a cult comes down to 4 common traits cults possess. All 4 of these signs must be present for it to be recognized as a cult.

Let's put the FIRE movement to the test through the lens of these 4 cult characteristics to determine which apply. (Note: This chapter was inspired by an article at Millennial-Revolution.com, a FIRE blog)

Characteristic #1: An ideology at odds with normal society

Cult members believe in non-traditional ideologies that the rest of society disagrees with. Often, these ideologies are considered weird or unusual by people outside the movement.

Further, members of a cult are often taught society is lying to them and only the Cult knows the truth. Inevitably, an "us vs. them" mentality emerges. You better do what the ideology teaches so that you can be protected from the enemy, who is constantly spreading lies. Does the FIRE movement do this?

For people seeking financial independence and early retirement, their ideology is definitely seen as non-traditional. Retiring at or around age 67 is traditional in the US. Most of society would disagree that you can or *should* aim to retire in your 50s, 40s, or even 30s. Instead, society pushes consumerism. However, individuals in the FIRE movement live on less and live with less. They inherently understand happiness doesn't come from spending money or owning things.

There is a bit of an "us vs. them" mentality when it comes to spending at your means vs. living below your means. It's not quite minimalism extreme in most cases, but it is seen as radical to most and FIRE seekers think over-spending or debt is irrational.

So yes, we can check off box one out of four. FIRE ideology is at odds with "normal" society. But does the FIRE movement check any more cult characteristics? Does it check all 4? Is it a cult? Let's find out…

Characteristic #2: An authoritarian leader

While not necessarily formally elected, most cults have a leader that they worship and follow blindly. This single leader makes the decisions and reinforces the ideals of the group. They have absolute power and are worshiped like a god in many cases. The leader cannot be questioned or challenged. They demand loyalty and may threaten and resort to violence if their authority is questioned.

Does the FIRE movement do this?

It's kind of a funny thing when it comes to the FIRE movement and leadership. While there's certainly zero chance of threats or violence, the FIRE movement does have a pseudo-leader. His name is Mr. Money Mustache. His followers consider themselves Mustachians. They even have a silly salute hand-gesture mustache thing. Plus, on his very own website, he literally calls himself the leader of the FIRE movement. It's very visible on the homepage near his email signup.

Who is this Mustachian man? Without going too far into it, Mr. Money Mustache runs a wildly popular blog in the FIRE community and many people (including myself) love to cite one of his articles in particular called The Shockingly Simple Math Behind Early Retirement. It's widely known as the first article that went viral and really put the FIRE movement on the map.

So again, yes, most would argue the FIRE movement has a leader that followers look up to and respect. Although it's nothing like what I described regarding absolute power and demanding loyalty, I'll go ahead and say FIRE is so far 2 for 4 when it comes to exhibiting the four cult-like characteristics. Right about now I'm starting to question that giant mustache I recently got tattooed across my back. I'm kidding of course…

Characteristic #3: Indoctrination and brainwashing

A big part of cults is recruitment and initiation so to speak. It's teaching new members the belief system, which is essentially training "us vs. them" thinking. During the learning or indoctrination phase, you're not allowed to question the information. You must follow the group leader blindly and always stay in line. Unfortunately, when it comes to cults, brainwashing occurs, which can happen in sinister and deceptive ways. Think of threats, violence, lies, and intimidation.

Does the FIRE movement do this?

Of course not. ABSOLUTELY NOT. In no way, shape, or form does this happen in the FIRE community. Yes, education is a big part of it. Math is a big part of it when it comes to investing, compound interest, and savings rates. But there is no singular path. In fact, there are infinite paths to achieving financial independence. There are near-infinite ways to seek early retirement.

Sharing unique paths and stories is a huge part of the financial independence culture. There's nothing competitive about it. The community absolutely encourages open conversations about money.

I enjoy reading different stories on Reddit. I follow and read a dozen FIRE blogs. I even enjoy reading contrarian beliefs, the naysayer's opinion, because it feels healthy to internalize all information and challenge myself from time to time. I'm constantly learning new things and that's what I love about running a finance YouTube channel and writing about personal finance—it keeps me honest and constantly researching. Again, this one is a resounding no. But there's one more to go. Will FIRE check 3 of the 4 boxes? Let's discuss...

Characteristic #4: Exploitation

Finally, the last characteristic of a cult is exploitation. The Money Revolution blog details exactly what this means.

The last, and most significant warning sign of a cult is the presence of exploitation. Specifically, every cult exists to exploit their members, either financially, physically, or sometimes sexually. Everything a cult does, presenting the dire world-view, creating a strong-man leader, and indoctrinating/brain-washing their members, is meant to persuade them to let themselves be exploited. Cult members will often give up their values, their relationships, and even their own identity when joining a cult. Their finances are usually completely controlled by the cult masters, and they cease to operate as an individual. Say goodbye to whatever money they had going in...

Does the FIRE movement do this?

This one is easy. This description is the furthest from any kind of description of people in the financial independence, retire early movement. In fact, I'd argue it's the exact opposite. The whole point of FIRE is to grow your wealth and do it quickly so you can enjoy a more free life where work becomes optional. It's about getting time back so you can pursue your passions, travel, try new hobbies, spend more time with kids and family, and (my personal favorite) sleep better at night.

Funny enough, people who have achieved FIRE have zero reasons to exploit anyone because they have a nest egg and they know this money will last them through retirement. They also understand "you can't take it with you." FIRE individuals have spent years learning to live happier lives with less. They've gained a better appreciation for the things that don't cost money in life to enjoy. Plus, they're earning passive income to help sustain them in retirement from investment gains and dividends at a minimum. For others like myself, I'm writing books, blogging, and I created my YouTube channel as passive income streams.

Again, no on this one. Yes, FIRE seekers want money because it's a tool to achieve financial freedom and independence. But no, they don't want yours. A final note on this: FIRE seekers give. They know the importance of giving, even when you have very little. I don't have any stats to back this up, but I would venture to guess they give far more than the average person.

FINAL THOUGHTS AND TAKEAWAYS

In the end, I've realized FIRE is definitely a cult… tural revolution in the finance space. I had you there for a second I hope! This exercise had me a little worried when I finished reading about the second characteristic but obviously #3 and #4 couldn't be further from what the FIRE movement is all about.

As with any group of people who go against the grain and think differently than the majority of society, there's going to be backlash and skepticism. There are going to be naysayers. I was absolutely one of them. In the Introduction of this book, I explained I was totally against it, but only because I was uneducated about it.

I thought all FIRE seekers saved 70% of their income at a *minimum*. Personally, I aim to save 50%. Others save 25–40% of their post-tax income. I thought the FIRE movement required becoming a minimalist and owning practically nothing. Some are minimalists. But many aren't. I thought FIRE seekers were missing out on the best years of their lives. I assumed they never traveled. I assumed they were judgemental. I assumed they were in some kind of cult.

Wrong, wrong, and wrong.

Today's movement vs. cult comparison helped me understand why I personally felt the way I did and I hope it was a little bit eye-opening for you. Here's what I've learned from comments from FIRE-seekers on my YouTube videos: They're open and honest and comfortable being vulnerable. They're the opposite of judgemental or stuffy. They're human. They're humans that simply want more out of life. Do you want to know why?

It's because we're not out to change anyone else's mind. We're here for one another and we genuinely enjoy hearing other people's stories and thoughts. Because we understand that together all of us, not only FIRE seekers, are greater than the sum of our parts.

Sports teams know this. Families know this. Teachers know this. Governments and religion, no matter where you stand on those, know this. Packs of wolves know this. Birds of a feather flock together, they say. That's all the FIRE community is. It's a group of people who think similarly, have similar goals, and are seeking a richer life. When I say "rich", it's not monetary, it's a sense of fulfillment.

I didn't wake up one day and decide to FIRE. If FIRE appeals to you, you're in. The reality is—you don't need an invitation to join. For me, it hit me one day when reading about it: *Wow, I already do all that. It's simply smart. I want to get to know this community more because we think alike.* If you're learning about FIRE, you don't have to go all in. Take the bits and pieces that work for you and your life and ignore what doesn't work. It's as simple as that.

CHAPTER TWENTY

Myths About the FIRE Community

Exhibit A: It's impossible to achieve FIRE

When it comes to the FIRE movement, there are common myths and misconceptions that people are simply wrong about. Quite frankly, I was wrong about a few FIRE ideas as well. In the next chapter we'll cover misconceptions. For now, let's start with myths. Here are ideas most people think about the FIRE movement that I found to be untrue:

- They're all minimalists that own nothing.
- They're not frugal, they're cheap.
- FIRE seekers are numbers nerds who obsess over budgets.
- There's only one FIRE path.
- It's impossible to achieve FIRE.

They're all minimalists that live in extreme frugality

The lifestyle seems extreme for many. Many in the FIRE community do save 25–70% of their income. However, they don't all identify as minimalists, and 25%-35% is not extreme. I own plenty of clothes, shoes, books, board games, tech, video games, and a few really nice household items we've invested in. I have two 4K TVs. I'm still able to save half.

FIRE seekers aim to live on less than the average American, so you don't *have* to work forever or work yourself to death. You don't *have* to trade your time for money. Living with less is part of it, but not near as much as many think.

This is worth repeating from earlier: *According to a TD Ameritrade and Harris Poll survey, the majority of financially independent survey respondents (67%) said FIRE isn't worth it if they have to live as though they're broke. 40% said they would limit travel or going on a vacation in regards to what they'd give up—similar to what people who hadn't achieved financial independence said.*

Yes, principles of minimalism do parallel or overlap with FIRE Movement principles, but it is certainly not a requirement. In fact, a recent phrase starting to catch popularity is financial minimalism. I'm not 100% sure how we define it yet, but for me, that means applying principles of minimalism to your finances. It's keeping things simple in terms of how many credit cards you have, your investments, and how you save. When you keep things simple, you're also keeping things organized, and I find that to be a reason I don't have to keep a budget. Speaking of...

They're all budgeters and numbers nerds

The truth is, most people aren't doing nearly enough to save towards retirement. They aren't on track. Most are far from being on track. So, budgeting is a great place to start. If nothing else, tracking your spending and setting up a budget for even a few months can be an eye-opening experience. Many people in the FIRE community budget. Some budget intensely to the penny. I don't.

I plan at the beginning of the year, and I automate my way to my goals with systems. Goals and systems help you set it and forget it. I don't have the time or desire to analyze every number. I don't want to analyze how every decision (spending or investing) will impact my target retirement date.

For those that do live by their spreadsheet, and there are quite a few, they should be applauded. I admire them because the truth is most Americans have ZERO budget, and this is a big reason why they're falling behind. Most don't know what they don't know because they don't track. At the end of each month, they wonder where the heck their money went and why they have nothing to show for their hard work.

My opinion is that budgets can be a good habit when starting out. Give it a shot, but there are other ways to save and cut expenses. For those of you doing what I do instead, which is to set up a plan at the beginning of the year and automate your way to your goals, nicely done as well. For those of you that are looking for a starting place to get your finances right, creating a budget is one of the best places to start. Maybe it's time you start tracking your spending by category.

They're not frugal, they're cheap

FIRE seekers only stream TV by using friends' logins. They never pick up the tab or tip above 10%. They definitely don't donate to charity because they hoard all of their money. And they definitely don't buy coffee. *Sarcasm intended.*

It's not that they are cheap, it's that they appreciate delayed gratification rather than needing to do everything now. They don't move from one shiny thing to the next like most of society. Instead, what's at the forefront of their thinking is that they are looking forward to several decades of doing what they want, when they want. Many people in the FIRE community give more than others. Most automate their giving. Some plan to give 10% of all income because they know that if you don't give now when you have little, you won't give when you have more or in retirement.

I'm not cheap, but I do pride myself on not paying full price for anything. Lots of non-FIRE people do the same. I use credit card rewards points when I can. I look for the best deal by comparison shopping. I take advantage of discounts and sales, but ONLY when it's something I've been wanting for a long time, not an impulsive purchase.

I find enjoyment in getting a good deal, but I also find enjoyment in tipping well and buying quality items at full price that will last a long time. By now, most of my friends know I'm conscious of spending habits, but I've never felt like they think I'm cheap. In fact, nowadays, I get text messages from friends asking where they can score the best deal for a big purchase because they too realize not paying full price feels really good. A penny saved is a penny earned. That mentality doesn't make you cheap. It makes you thoughtful.

There's one path

FIRE seekers aren't perfect with money. Nobody is. Yes, you'll get there sooner if you save half or more, but it isn't totally necessary. There are constantly new paths based on new stories, tax laws, evolving strategies, and more.

There's definitely no one-size-fits-all plan. I would even argue there's no one-size-fits-most plan. Like with sports, or trying to lose weight, or learning how to cook, or training for a job—there are best practices. Ultimately, it's up to you to learn and take what applies to you and your goals to implement it. FIRE does mean being a lifetime learner that adapts.

You can try to earn more or spend less. You can pay off debts or invest. You can focus on reducing the big 3: housing, food, and transportation. You could invest in rental properties and become a landlord. You could play the credit card points game. Some utilize geoarbitrage where they keep their big-city income, but work remotely in a low cost of living area, possibly abroad. FIRE seekers resist impulse purchases. They aim to live well below their means. But outside of that, the journeys are all unique, as they should be.

FIRE doesn't work

It's unrealistic. It won't work for most people. There's no point in trying. 25 times your expenses are NOT enough. Living off of 4% of your portfolio isn't enough. Medical expenses are way too high in old age. Kid's colleges need to be paid for. Emergencies happen. *I'm channeling my inner Suze Orman right now…*

I recently listened to a podcast episode on the Afford Anything podcast with Paula Pant where Suze criticized the movement. It was shocking. And truthfully, a bit upsetting because she's completely missing the point and the good in the community.

The principles are good and do work. Seeking early retirement gives people a goal at the very least. It teaches people how to get out of debt and increase their savings rate. It makes investing simple, so they actually do it. It gives people hope—real hope that's a million times more likely to happen than winning the lottery, which millions of people waste money on.

FIRE seekers learn how to pay fewer taxes by taking maximum advantage of tax-advantaged retirement accounts available. It's making yourself recession-proof by building up a strong emergency fund. It's giving and paying it forward. It's building community and support. FIRE shows that anyone can reject the status quo and seek more out of their life, no matter who they are. It shows we don't need a million things to be happy.

People seeking FIRE value experiences: Spending time with loved ones, reading, and learning, traveling, living a healthy lifestyle where they make their own food with good ingredients. Plus, thousands upon thousands of people have retired early. There is proof. Countless examples of it. Many have retired in their early 30s. Some in their 50s, which is still early and gives you 15 years of your time back to spend with kids and grandkids or travel. I assure you, it's not a pipe dream. Anybody can do it because it's not about how much money you make; it's how much you're able to save (your savings rate) that matters most.

They retire and do nothing

75% of financially independent respondents from that TD American study said financial security is more important than retiring early. Only 35% said they were motivated by the prospect of leaving a 40-hour-a-week job. People overwhelmingly said they were simply looking for work/life balance.

Many that retire early find work they love. It may not be full-time work. In many cases, they start their own company. They earn some sort of income that takes the pressure off of relying solely on their Freedom Fund. Many build passive income streams and live off of that until they can tap into retirement accounts without penalty.

I imagine I'll continue to write and put in countless hours on my YouTube channel in "retirement" because I love it. That's the point. FIRE means freedom to pursue a passion — one that still likely contributes to society. The truth is, it's the "RE" part of "FIRE," the "retire early" part, that irks some and causes all the controversy. It's a clever acronym, but I wish RE was left off. People in the FIRE Movement are seeking financial independence when they no longer *have* to exchange their time for money. I wish they had called it FIOR: Financial Independence, Optional Retirement.

FINAL THOUGHTS AND TAKEAWAYS

The finance media *loves* to talk about the FIRE Movement; some positive, but mainly in a negative light. People in the FIRE community all have extremely interesting and compelling stories, the kind of stories that make you think: *how the heck do they do that* or *why the heck do they do that?* Unfortunately, it's the negative click-bait headlines that steal the spotlight.

But the best part of the movement that those headlines miss is the community—the support system. It's people that all want the same thing: *freedom*. It's people who think differently. People that look for a different path than the status-quo. They don't accept having to work for 45 years, punching in 9–5 Monday through Friday at a job you may not love or have passion for. They deny hoping to fit in a vacation. Hoping for a raise. Hoping for a bonus. Hoping for a positive performance review.

"FIOR" seekers don't get distracted by the Joneses or spending impulsively because everyone else is doing it. They reject money as a taboo topic to discuss, even if that's how it was in their house growing up. They encourage conversations about consumer debts or student loans. They refuse to accept the "I'll deal with it later mentality" or a "kick the can down the road" mentality.

Choosing FI means symbolically joining a community of people that want more out of life. And almost none of them retire or stop working. Most of them pay it forward, share what they learn, and offer to help others on their journey. And all of them are beautiful, smart, intelligent people. People that should be congratulated and admired. It's people that inspire me and hopefully now, maybe you.

CHAPTER TWENTY-ONE

FIRE Movement Misconceptions

FIRE isn't for everyone, but it can be for anyone

It seems trendy to bash the FIRE movement in the media. I've come across a lot of negative articles and videos on the topic—especially the "why we quit the FIRE movement" variety. They say any publicity is good publicity, and the FIRE movement overall has gained significant media attention recently. It sure doesn't feel like good publicity...

Google trends for "Financial Independence Retire Early" have massively increased in the last 5 years, but it's clear in browsing results that there are still serious misconceptions about FIRE. Many people don't understand or appreciate the full concept of FIRE. I want to clear some of that up while offering some motivating advice no matter where you are on your journey—whether you consider yourself a part of the movement or not. Because nobody can deny there are a lot of great financial practices FIRE seekers believe in that would help anybody improve their financial situation.

They save 80% or more of their income and live on rice and beans

There's a wide spectrum when it comes to people's savings rate within the FIRE movement. It could be as "little" as 15 to 20% or as much as 80 or 85% on the more extreme side. The 80%+ crew probably lives with their parents or paid off a mortgage, or are high-income earners ($150,000+). It's a small minority, yet they are often reported on.

FIRE is about how quickly you're trying to achieve financial independence. Obviously, the more you save, the less you spend. Therefore, you can get to your FIRE number where work becomes optional sooner.

For me, I split the difference. I started way behind at nearly 6-figures in debt at age 31. First, I got to 25% saving rate, then 35% in year 2, and 50% in years 3 and 4. I found the sweet spot for me at 50% and encourage people to get there if possible. But you should never feel like you only eat rice and beans to get by on your journey. In fact, I made a YouTube video that discusses the benefits of splurge spending.

Most in the FIRE movement don't feel put out. An Ameritrade study found that extreme lifestyle sacrifices are actually less common among FIRE devotees. 67% of study participants said FIRE wouldn't be worth it if they had to live like they're broke. Instead, FIRE is all about experimentation. You need to find what feels most comfortable month to month. You have lots of levers to pull and tinker with—how much you save or invest, trying out a budget, reducing expenses, avoiding fees, automation, and even extreme frugality for a short time.

They're running away from work and their job.

If you're looking to get on the FIRE path because you simply hate your job, you're doing it wrong. FIRE isn't about running from something—it's about running towards something. For more than 70% of survey respondents, financial independence is their main pursuit instead of retirement itself. And over 60% said they would prefer to retire at a normal age so they can live more comfortably. Only 32% of respondents said their goal was to stop working altogether.

For most, reaching financial independence does not mean the end of work. In fact, most people want to achieve FI, so they can pursue a passion or try a unique career that feels risky as a 9 to 5. It could be starting a business, turning a hobby into a gig, or simply working less. The retire early part of the FIRE acronym is the part the naysayers get hung upon. Perhaps R.E. is only part of the acronym because saying FIRE is catchy and "retire early" is a clear, desirable goal for many people.

Yes, it likely means an escape from a traditional 9 to 5, including traffic, meetings, KPIs, and daily small talk. However, most FIRE seekers still plan to work hard at something that is important to them. It could be work for money and/or work for passion, but one thing is true: they don't quit contributing to society in some way, shape, or form.

It's impossible on a low or even moderate-income

Being on the FIRE path isn't only for 6-figure earners and up. While you might hear of the $200,000 a year techie retiring in less than 10 years, it's not the most common FIRE path. Instead, it's everyday people, even low-income earners, living below their means and achieving their goals a decade or more sooner than the average person.

It doesn't matter how much money you make. It's your savings rate and investing that matters the most. It's not that a super low-income earner can magically retire in 5 or 10 years, but retiring 10 years before the average person is extremely doable for anyone. Anyone, on any income, can make their lives better by spending less on things that don't improve their lives.

On the opposite end, many high-income earners struggle to manage their money well. 40% percent of high-earners are still living paycheck to paycheck. Earning more makes it easy to let lifestyle inflation creep into your life. You constantly upgrade and become used to a certain amount of annual spending. That makes it very difficult to retire early because you won't have practice living off of a modest, or even average, income. Bottom line: FIRE is simply a personal math exercise. As stated before, running numbers through a retirement calculator is one way to see and understand compound interest and how possible achieving FI is. Mr. Money Mustache said it best when he wrote:

"At the core, these FIRE ideas are simply about taking some solid math, combining it with principles of human happiness, and then distilling it down into a list of simple tactics that will get you way ahead in all areas of life. The benefits go way beyond money."

For more on achieving FIRE on a low income, we'll deep dive into this concept in Chapter 25.

They're obsessed with the FIRE movement and accumulating wealth

People that consider themselves FIRE don't eat, sleep and breathe FIRE. I don't, and I have a mostly FIRE channel on YouTube that keeps me really engaged with the movement a couple of days a week. Happiness and freedom are the goals of FIRE. That's what people get obsessed with. Over 90% of financially independent individuals say that happiness is more important than money. I found financial freedom starts to be realized far before reaching financial independence. I view it as a state of being.

I only read one personal finance book so far in 2021. I've been enjoying mindset, productivity, leadership, and entrepreneurship books instead. I'm doing this intentionally. I recognized I need balance —everything in moderation, even seeking financial independence. Happiness is far more important than wealth. It so happens, in the society we live in, money causes a lot of stress and anxiety. Therefore, FIRE seekers want to put that anxiety to bed by getting on the path, but they aren't in a hurry. That said, you can solve a good chunk of your biggest money issues 2 to 3 years into your financial independence journey.

Plus, once you learn the basics and set yourself up for success, it's pretty easy to stay on the path passively. You don't have to be perfect to be FIRE. You'll make mistakes. You might switch paths. Life happens, and you'll need to adjust. But it's best to aim big and implement the basics. The core principles are easier to grasp and implement than most realize. Reaching FI will likely take decades to achieve for most people where work becomes optional. FIRE seekers have to practice patience and keep a long-term perspective. You certainly can't FIRE overnight.

You also can't force FIRE on anyone. FIRE seekers know this. FIRE seekers aren't obsessed. They're simply determined to solve their money problems so they can seek a richer, as in happier, life.

FIRE is only for young people that don't have kids

Financial independence is for anyone, on any income, at any age. Obviously, you can't retire early if you're 60 with a net worth of $50,000 or less. But you can set yourself up to enjoy a standard retirement following FIRE principles.

Tons of people over 50 discover FIRE and realize the FIRE path could help make up for decades of financial mistakes made. They realized there is still hope, and it doesn't mean extreme living. They already have the urgency and desire, and FIRE can be that beacon of hope. Anecdotally, I've heard those over 50 in the FIRE movement on the path are the most enthusiastic. Typically I say "save and invest half, retire twice as fast" because you can retire in as little as 17 years if you save 50% of your after-tax income. But if you're in your mid-50s and discovering FIRE and feel behind, remember: "Save and invest half and grind; there's still a great chance you'll retire on time."

In terms of kids and a family—yes, kids cost money. But, from what I hear, the reports about the costs of having a single kid in his or her lifetime are grossly overreported. Not to mention, those seeking FIRE understand the importance of saving for big expenses for their kids. An example is paying for higher education via 529 plans for growth and tax benefits. Having kids is what turns many people onto the FIRE movement in the first place. They want the freedom to spend more time with their kids. Then they discover an alternative FIRE path like Coast FIRE or Barista FIRE, and they run the numbers and realize they can make it happen sooner than they thought. Kids and less time both equal more motivation.

If you can get the whole family on board with living below their means, practicing frugality, and learning to appreciate family and shared experiences more than tangible things, you're doing great! Plus, it's an excellent life lesson to teach kids and family to save together.

They don't know how to loosen up, have fun, and live in the moment

The whole reason for seeking FIRE is to lead the happiest, most satisfying life you can possibly lead. That's now in the present, as well as the future. Indulge when and where you can, but know your level of happiness isn't tied to things or stuff or drinks or going out for coffee and meals daily.

Happiness comes from meeting certain core human needs, and there are countless ways to meet each of those needs—many of which don't cost any money.

The "I deserve it" indulgence is what gets many people in trouble. Not knowing how to say no or resist temptations gets people in trouble and in debt. Most of these are short-term pleasures that distract from long-term goals. Heck, most people get into a financial debt mess and don't consider setting financial goals at all.

FIRE has given me a new appreciation for new kinds of affordable fun: exercising, reading, taking my dog to the park, listening to podcasts on daily walks, cooking meals with my partner, making videos, blogging, and watching the sunrise or sunset.

There are many ways to accomplish tasks or have fun affordably. FIRE seekers are creative thinkers. They find ways to get what they want for cheap so they can enjoy it even more. I wrote a whole book about money hacks, because I get genuine enjoyment from earning a discount, scoring free tickets to an event, browsing Buy Nothing groups, playing the credit card points game, or hosting friends for game night.

The alternative sounds so much worse: Throw money in every direction in a constant chase of dopamine hits without considering goals while living paycheck to paycheck. Dizzying, to say the least. Distractions lead to more debt, less freedom, and less free time later on. Debt or saving zero is robbing you of your future.

They don't have backup plans

First of all, FIRE seekers believe in and prioritize building an emergency fund as a core principle to be prepared for almost anything. They typically aim to have at least a year of expenses on hand. In terms of a backup plan—well, there's always working longer or going back to work. That's the beauty of it. It's not black and white. Work, then don't work. Then work again if you get bored or need to. Work will always be there. But time with family, good health, and energy to travel—those can be fleeting, so it's all about aligning priorities with what's most important to you.

FIRE seekers believe every problem can be solved, and financial independence gives you more power to solve these problems. FIRE attracts the kind of people that are willing to do what it takes to achieve success and happiness but not at all costs obsessively. The truth is, those in the FIRE movement don't have everything figured out, but the community is always there for support and ideas. They are all about lifting one another up and working through it together. It truly is a community, ready to help, without arrogance or judgment. It's far better than not talking money with anyone because it's a taboo topic—the reality for most.

Nothing is permanent. Not even staying retired. But most people don't consider any other plan other than retirement at the standard age when their physical and mental health will not be at their peak. I love hearing early retiree stories saying they are living their glory years at age 45 or 55. I used to dread getting older. Now I look forward to it.

FINAL THOUGHTS AND TAKEAWAYS

Rant time because I get fired up about this topic (pun intended). FIRE has spread in popularity because it works, but criticism has also spread because others aren't willing to look under the hood. They'd rather misunderstand it, report on extreme cases, and share negativity about it because it's different from societal norms. Perhaps what's normal is *wrong*.

What's normal about going into thousands of dollars of debt because of loud advertisements and trying to impress people you don't care about with toys and things that depreciate in value rapidly? What's normal about rolling the dice financially for decades, living on the edge, and hoping you'll figure it out or get bailed out later on? What's normal about schools not teaching us even the basics when it comes to personal finance, then providing $100,000 in student loans to an 18-year-old without credit that will take 30 years to pay it off, $250,000 later? What's normal about not setting future goals and limiting your beliefs when it comes to creating generational wealth, providing a better life for your kids than you had growing up, and enjoying life on your own terms? What's normal about sitting at a work desk in your 50s and 60s instead of seeing the world or doing things you've always dreamed of doing because you feel stuck financially?

I'll tell you what's normal about it all... nothing. I'm certainly biased since I'm on the FIRE path, but I'm not here to convince anyone to join the movement. Instead, I'm here to provide content and context that helps when people decide they're tired of the status quo that's practically designed to keep most people broke.

If you want more out of your life and want more of your hard work and earnings to go further and grow, instead of disappearing shortly after each payday, consider checking out my YouTube channel. I keep it actionable, relatable, fun, and very honest. I'll never say the FIRE path is the perfect path of rainbows and happiness. I will say, I'm 5 times happier than I was 5 years ago when I was drowning in debt, depressed about it, and silent about it.

But alas, there are actual downsides of chasing your FIRE dreams. We need to confront and internalize these downsides with honesty and transparency because the path will inevitably have it's bumps and challenges. It's more difficult if you aren't prepared and these challenges are unexpected.

CHAPTER TWENTY-TWO

Is FIRE Worth It?

This is what they don't tell you about financial independence

It's the RE side of the FIRE acronym that carries a negative connotation and can rub people the wrong way. Perhaps for good reason. I discovered FIRE in 2018, in my year of turning my financial life around. For years, I was one of those people that scoffed at the notion of FIRE. But one day, I realized: *I essentially am following all or most of the FIRE principles.* All of my reading, research, and actions led me down a path that made clear sense to me. I have no doubt anyone would benefit from some or all of the principles the FIRE community preaches.

But what am I missing? Is there a blind spot I'm not seeing? What are the real drawbacks of retiring early? These are the cons I found that anyone on the FIRE path or considering early retirement should be aware of. However, I'm not here to simply wave red flags and offer ominous warnings. In the end, I'll leave you with a handful of useful ideas and helpful suggestions to reframe some of your thinking so you can enjoy the journey *and* the destination a little bit more.

You might get really, really bored and lonely

Most of your closest friends, family members, and former colleagues are still on the clock from 9 to 5, Monday through Friday. You might be retired early. But they aren't... It sounds a lot like the first time you pretended you were sick so you could stay home from school. That first hour or two of playing video games or watching movies was great. But the feeling wore off as you started to wonder what your friends were doing without you at school.

See also: Self-quarantining. It was fun working from home and doing puzzles daily… for about a month. It's funny how quickly that wore off. We all had a decrease in social (and likely physical) activities for a year or more. We learned how social isolation could negatively impact us, and that can be a real thing in early retirement as well.

You're going to need more than a hobby. You'll need several hobbies or a big passion project. You'll need active hobbies. And I hope you have affordable hobbies because…

Your expenses might actually go up

This one sounds counterintuitive at first glance, but it's true. An obvious reason why is because you'll have more time on your hands and people spend money when they're bored. Furthermore, early retirement is the perfect time to travel. I could easily see this turning into a bit of an addiction. If money and work weren't a factor, I myself would love to travel a third of the year or more.

It's easy to say no to little things or unnecessary purchases when you're on the FIRE path. You have a huge end goal you're working towards. You also understand the power of time in the market when it comes to investing. In early retirement, you're at the "end goal." You did it. You worked so hard for this, so enjoy it! Buy the thing. Do the experience. Stop wasting time to score the best deal. Live it up! Donate more. Gift better. Start that expensive hobby you've always dreamed of. I'm not saying this happens to everyone, but it certainly seems very plausible.

Then there's the dreaded "H" word, the biggie: healthcare.

You'll need to find healthcare. And it can be pricey.

Insurance premiums can easily be double or triple what you're used to paying at work when your company is no longer picking up part of the tab. Health insurance rates climb as you get older and can reach four figures monthly after age 55. Healthcare will likely be your #1 expense in the latter part of your life. In terms of physical health, it can go both ways: Some focus on their health, and it improves dramatically. For others, it declines dramatically as people become less active or deal with emotional tolls I'm highlighting today.

Sam Dogen of the Financial Samurai said (USA Today): "It's an absurd amount of money. Either way you cut it, paying for unsubsidized health care is extremely expensive in America." He explained he pays over $21,000 a year out of pocket for his family of 3. Ouch. Healthcare in early retirement is a massive topic, and I can't give it the attention it deserves here, but it's a MUST know if you're on the FIRE path and something you need to consider years before reaching your early retirement goals.

You may suffer from an identity crisis

So… what do you do for a living? It's the question almost everybody asks when you meet them, without hesitation. If you're 45 and retired and you haven't thought of an answer to this question, it might catch you totally off guard.

On the one hand, you could respond that you're retired. But there's a fear that people might look at you funny or treat you differently, or even judge you. On the other hand, you could describe a hobby or passion you're working on with this newfound extra time, but that often leads to more questions and probably people looking at you funny.

Many struggle with personal identity in early retirement because our jobs are oftentimes a huge part of our identity. Our job is how people know us, and it represents how we contribute to society. You may not feel the same amount of respect if you feel others deem you too good to contribute towards society as a part of the working class. And that means something.

I used to love telling people I was a high school teacher, but two years removed from that, I was a lowly social media specialist at a local jewelry company. I avoided this interaction at all costs. People might think your early retirement is awesome—but most won't understand or care to learn.

You may second-guess yourself

Maybe you didn't make the right decision. Maybe there's this weird part of you that starts to miss corporate life and constantly seeing the people there. In fact, in a 2017 CompHealth survey, 68% of the 400 late-career physicians surveyed said they were not excited about retirement. Some of the top concerns included losing social interactions at work, a loss of purpose, boredom, and depression.

Loss of motivation is common if you aren't retiring TO something. It becomes harder and harder to not hit snooze. In fact, *why set the alarm at all?* Here's why: When our brains rest, they rust. This is partly why people become physically unhealthy. Humans thrive with routine. If you don't work on creating routines in your life in early retirement, you'll get rusty.

Maybe that's why Mike Tyson recently fought again at age 54. He's out there knocking the rust off while others are sleeping in. If all you think about is early retirement as an end destination, it's going to get difficult on the other side. If you don't plan ahead and find a routine, you'll meet regret. And Regret is a jerk of a friend.

You may not be happier

People who win the lottery return to their same level of happiness months after. The same has been found to be true of people who lose an arm or a leg. They, too, adjust and return to the same level of happiness as before. This is known as the hedonic treadmill. We tend to want more and more without asking, *"how much is enough?"* Or we think "enough" equals happiness. I would argue "enough" means liberation from stress about money. But not stress overall.

It's like the letdown you might feel immediately after finishing the series finale of your favorite show or finishing a book you love. It's like Tom Brady preparing for next season, a day removed from winning his 7th super bowl. He's never satisfied.

Money won't solve all your problems, but it can solve your money problems. However, if you were unhappy before in your job, in early retirement, you simply have more time to sit and wallow in your unhappiness. Early retirement itself is not a purpose or a hobby. It helps you facilitate those, but it's not the end game to happiness. Remember, when it comes to retirement—it does not automatically equal a newfound level of happiness. That's because: Wherever you go, there you are.

Your Social Security benefits could be smaller

In the US, the sooner you start to take Social Security, the lower your benefits will be. If you were born in 1960 or later, for example, and you start taking benefits at age 62 (the earliest age at which you're eligible), your monthly benefits will be 30% less than if you wait until age 67, which Social Security refers to as your "full retirement age."

For each year you postpone from age 67 to 70, you'll receive an additional 8% in your monthly benefit. This is all to say, if you start tapping your social security benefits early, there will be fewer benefits overall for you. This whole social security thing is kind of a mess though, so I'll leave it at that. Funding early retirement can be complicated, especially if you have most of your assets in retirement accounts you can't access without penalty.

How to avoid these common early retirement downsides

First off, it's critical you retire *to* something, not *from* something. Don't run from a job you hate. That's not the reason people seek early retirement. Run towards a life you love. *That's* the core of FIRE.

Here are more ways to live happy in early retirement:

- Have a healthy social life. Make this a priority.
- Keep your mind and body active. Take a hike or nature walk.
- Focus on earning passive income doing something you love.
- Try a reduced work schedule like moving to a part-time job before taking the leap to retire completely.

- Take an active role in your local community. For example, I'd love to coach little league or get back in the classroom as a part-time substitute teacher.
- Pursue FIRE with a partner or best friend. Travel together. Be alive together.
- Share your journey. Write about it. Join FIRE communities and engage. Be open and honest about your wins and struggles.
- It's never too late to be a part of the workforce if you so choose to. FIRE means work is optional. Keyword: *optional*.

Finally, don't let judgment or the fear of judgment hold you back because here's a reality: if people are judging, they're likely jealous. Here's another reality: most people don't care about your lifestyle. They're too busy caring about themselves. There's no singular FIRE path or right and wrong way to enjoy early retirement. Do it your way. Either way, I want to double down and remind you to connect with like-minded people. The community part of FIRE is, in my opinion, the best part. It's people that want to challenge the status quo. People that want more out of life. People that are willing to work hard to achieve their goals and are willing to go out of their way to help others. Remember, there's no such thing as THE path. There's only *your* path. Best of luck no matter what you're running *towards*.

CHAPTER TWENTY-THREE

Burnt Out? You Might Need A Mini-Retirement

Consider shaking it up by stepping away from work

Let me be clear: this chapter isn't meant to convince you to quit your job and take extended time off ASAP. My goal is to expand your thinking, share an interesting idea, and help you think creatively when it comes to your financial life. Or should I say: *your life*. This is your life, and you have more control over it than you might realize—a mini-retirement is one idea that proves that. Perhaps there is an alternative to the traditional path or working for 45 years, retiring at age 67, and hoping you're healthy enough to enjoy it.

What is a mini-retirement?

A mini-retirement is when you take time away from work for an extended period. It's intentional and requires planning in advance. The term was coined by Tim Ferris in his book *The 4-Hour Workweek*. He called it: *"A series of meaningful respites throughout your life in which you take a break (or breaks) from your career, rather than just one final one at the end."*

This isn't saving up vacation hours and sick days and taking a month off. This isn't necessarily a sabbatical. This isn't extending maternity or paternity time because you want more time with your newborn. Do those things if you desire, but the difference is a mini-retirement should be a well-thought-out plan, funded and communicated clearly to work and discussed transparently with loved ones.

If you do it this way, it can be self-reflective and eye-opening. Maybe even life-changing. For the right person in the right situation, a mini-retirement can be an incredibly refreshing and rewarding experience.

In a 2014 study by Project Time Off, they found that 95% of respondents knew the value of taking time off, but more than 40% of respondents leave paid time off on the table annually. The study also revealed 25% of people view their jobs as the primary source of stress in their lives. Does this sound familiar? Oftentimes, it's fear that gets in our way. Many are worried that taking time off will make you look less committed, your work will pile up, you'll look replaceable, or it'll slow down your odds of a promotion.

But here's the kicker: The study also found that employees who take time away from work for a more extended period come back feeling mentally refreshed, energized, and overall more productive and happier. Plus, that happiness extends beyond work, AND they end up *more* financially secure. Fundamentally, we all know that *time off is good for you. Breaks are necessary.* Is extended time off good for you and necessary? Only you can decide.

Who is a mini-retirement for?

As much as I talk about and support striving for early retirement, I fully realize that it simply may not be feasible for everyone, and there are some obvious drawbacks.

Traditional society wants us to work roughly 45 years, save and invest, so we can enjoy doing what we want to do at age 67 or later. But is good health guaranteed at 67? Will you have the same amount of energy to travel or buy and fix up a car, or go sailing, or even run around with grandkids then? I don't mean to be morbid, but reaching age 67 isn't fully guaranteed. Even if you chase early retirement and retire at age 45, by then, you might have a family yourself. That's another reason you might want to consider a mini-retirement.

A mini-retirement is potentially for you if you have big plans for what you want to personally do or accomplish in life—things you want to do before you have a family, before the grey hairs, and before knee and back pain starts "creaking" in.

A mini-retirement is potentially for you if you want to spend a year traveling or have always considered working part-time abroad. It's for you if you need a serious battery recharge because you're feeling burnt out by your current job. I was a high school teacher for four years. I changed careers because of burnout. Maybe I didn't need a new career. *Maybe I needed time off.* Mini-retirement could be for you if you know you have an idea for a book or business, but know you really need space and time to reflect and create. It might be for you if you're going through a really tough time personally. Think death in the family, divorce, or health issues.

Mini-retirement might be for you if you have a baby on the way, money set aside, and extended time off has been the plan all along. Finally, it could be you if you're simply in a funk and need something new and exciting to look forward to. It can be time to reset, refresh and figure out your next move.

Who isn't a mini-retirement for?

Mini-retirement is not for people who are sick and tired of work and have a poor work ethic. It's not for people looking for an escape or excuse to quit tomorrow. It's not for people who don't have a plan or even a plan to have a plan. Mini-retirement is not a solution to all life's problems. It could set you back more if you don't plan accordingly, so let's discuss how to plan for it, what it looks like during it, and how to plan to reintegrate back into full-time work.

How do you plan for one?

Step 1: Plan and set a budget.

Know your current expenses and calculate your expenses during mini-retirement, especially if you're planning to travel. The last thing you want is to be totally unprepared financially. While the saving goal might be relatively simple to figure out, it won't be easy to achieve, of course, you likely need to save aggressively for a year or years. That's okay. Part of the fun is finally knowing there's that light at the end of the current daily grind tunnel.

Step 2: Consider setting up multiple passive income streams.

Set yourself up to earn income outside of your full-time gig. This could be from a rental property, investing, ebooks, courses, a YouTube channel, or selling digital products. This will help you fund or even extend your mini-retirement. Plus, it'll help you stay on track for full retirement.

Pro Tip: Consider developing your passive income during mini-retirement.

Step 3: Communicate with work.

Do not notify work the moment you're ready to start a mini-retirement. You should mention the idea as soon as a year before your extended time off. Then, check-in 6 months later. Finally, start making a firm ask 2 to 3 months out. Perhaps they will allow you to take a sabbatical or unpaid leave.

Extended time off is common in academia, but it's even becoming more common in the corporate world. A "career break," if you will. Keeping your job is not a guarantee, of course. If work does not guarantee a position when you return, you'll have a difficult decision to make. The sooner you introduce the idea, the better your odds. For some, however, a new job on the other side is part of the purpose.

Step 4: Remember your financial responsibilities.

I alluded to this when discussing passive income and retirement. Plan ahead so you can stay on track for your long-term financial goals. This could be full retirement, saving and investing consistently, saving for a child's college, or building up an emergency fund (which you should avoid touching during mini-retirement).

If your plan is to travel, consider this: traveling without purpose gets boring fast. New scenery is good but pursuing a passion, hobby, or goal is even better and *necessary*. Otherwise, you're the same YOU in a different location. Of course, you don't have to have it all figured out ahead of time. There's no singular path or plan.

"You may find that the most valuable part of your mini-retirement is the realization that you are your true security. You have strength and resiliency in reserve that you never knew about, and you must move out of your comfort zone in order to claim it." -Coach Carson

You don't have to have it all figured out, especially if it's your first mini-retirement. Trust your instincts.

What does it look like to return to "the real world"?

If you planned correctly, your job *might* be waiting for you. For most people, this isn't super likely. It's important you leave some budget for a month or two of expenses to find a job when you're ready to "un-retire." That's cash on hand—not invested where you might trigger taxable events if you sell or even lose money in the market.

You might want to consider freelancing, consulting, or other side gigs to pay the bills and get back in a rhythm. If you're lucky, you can take the skills you learned and a fresh perspective to pursue your own business. If you did work on building passive income streams, you might be able to keep work optional. This is difficult to accomplish, but a fantastic goal to strive towards.

Either way, have a plan and consistently strive towards fulfilling it so that 6 months or 1 year of time off doesn't delay full retirement by 2, 3, 5 years, or more. Never put your long-term success at risk. If you do, you're doing it wrong.

FINAL THOUGHTS AND TAKEAWAYS

It might sound difficult to land a new job with a gap in their resume.

Don't let this discourage you. Many people have gaps. Common reasons are: having a newborn, going back to school, traveling, and pursuing a business. Plus, it may make you a unique candidate with a great story—one that shows creativity, passion, and promise. Imagine the stories you'll tell when you do land that interview.

Finally, some pros and cons…

Pros of mini-retirements

- Mini-retirements might offer the best of both worlds. You can achieve a short-term goal by saving and planning, and you have the freedom of choice far before traditional retirement.
- You get away from the routine that doesn't allow for any time to stop, breathe, look around, and really reflect on what you have and what you want out of life.
- You might learn who you really are, what you really want, how to follow your instincts, and how to go against the grain.
- You might find work or a passion that's more fun, whether it provides a paycheck or not.

Con of mini-retirements

- If you don't have a plan and you don't plan ahead financially, it can become a disaster and set you way back, delaying retirement.
- It could slow down or derail your career progression. It would be tough to leave a job when you know you're in line for a promotion.
- You might develop new stress if you travel to an unknown place and find yourself in over your head or extremely homesick.
- You might realize you're simply running away from something (work) instead of running towards something like finding a hobby or passion or fulfilling a life-long dream.
- It's possible you experience a new, deeper sense of regret or depression when you return to work. The Monday blues,

multiplied by 10.

A quick tip to get you started: *Take a week off. Use that week, even at home, to reflect. Read. Learn. Side hustle. During that week, or if you're feeling ambitious for a month, stay off of social media. I recommend this as a tip during a real mini-retirement as well.*

Again, I don't want to encourage anyone out there to simply quit a job without a plan. I simply hope this helped expand your thinking. Perhaps this gives you hope and a short-term goal that will actually motivate you to get serious about saving and investing and eventually help you find your passion. As we learned earlier, most people reported feeling refreshed and reenergized and were more productive and happier after time off.

Imagine what you might feel like with a year off or more…

Don't forget: You don't have to choose between mini-retirements and retiring early. They can both work well together with thoughtful planning. The truth is, maybe having a plan is all you needed in the first place. It's important to hear different perspectives, learn about different paths, and consider different options when it comes to achieving financial freedom.

Part V

How to FIRE

CHAPTER TWENTY-FOUR

How to Achieve FIRE In A Big City

Never underestimate going back to basics

To achieve financial independence, you should aim to save half of your income. I wrote about why this is important and how to do it in previous chapters. You may be thinking: *Sure, half sounds great, but how can I save half if I live in an expensive city like New York or San Francisco?* I get it! Saving half can seem like a huge, overwhelming goal—especially when you live in a big city where rents and the housing market are rising year after year.

In fact, according to a recent survey by TD Ameritrade, nearly half of Americans say that the rising cost of living is the greatest threat to their financial security. Common advice from people pursuing FIRE is to move to a less expensive area. However, you may need to live in a big city to pursue your passion or profession. Or maybe you simply prefer living somewhere that happens to be expensive. I personally advocate for making choices that make you happy, not choosing your lifestyle based on what's cheapest. Here are actionable tips to get on the path to saving half of your post-tax income for financial independence in a big, expensive city.

Housing

Housing is typically your biggest expense and the one that people living in expensive cities can really struggle to keep down. In a high cost of living area, it is especially important to be smart about housing. Personally, I feel renting is hugely underrated. It is a great way to go if you live in a big city. You have the flexibility to move, and you save money by not having to pay for maintenance and repairs. However, even if you do rent, you can easily spend *way* too much on housing if you aren't smart about it.

Before I committed to getting better with money, I lived in a studio apartment by myself in one of the most expensive neighborhoods in Seattle. Not smart. Not only was it expensive, but it was also cramped. I literally had to sleep in my closet!

If you live in an expensive city, you should absolutely live with a partner, friend, or roommate as long as you can comfortably. I found my most recent apartment when I stopped in to buy a vacuum from a stranger on Craigslist. When I realized that the person was moving, I went to the leasing office and was able to get the apartment before it even went on the market at a great rate with some negotiating. With persistence and creativity, finding a good deal on housing is definitely possible!

Public transportation

If you live in a city with good public transit, use it. Personally, I use a combination of my moped and public transportation. I am consistently impressed by how clean and on-time the buses are. Reduce paying for gas and parking. Take the bus instead.

My company also offers a free transit pass, which is pretty common for companies in downtown Seattle. Make sure to ask about this type of perk when interviewing. And if your company offers a free or discounted pass, take full advantage of it!

Also, when you are looking for housing, be sure to factor in transportation costs. You may be able to save money by living in a neighborhood that is farther out. However, if it doesn't have great access to public transportation, you might end up driving (and spending more in both time and money).

Never pay full price

Always look for a discount. *Everything* is negotiable. Even rent as I mentioned. I treat it like a game. It can be fun to search for the best happy hour deals, coupons on your favorite foods, and welcome email offers for discounts on clothes or gadgets. When shopping online, I use Honey or set up alerts through Brad's Deals.

If I see something new that I want, I will wait a few months and then look for it used on Craigslist. As a bonus, I sometimes forget what I wanted to buy months later, which begs the question, did I really want it? It's nice sometimes to wait and think about that "want" after a few weeks or months, then knowing I didn't actually want it as much as I did months ago. Need a dog-sitter? Ask a friend and offer to do the same when they go away. Again, it's all about getting creative. Barter. Trade. And save all day!

Cheap thrills

Take advantage of all the free or cheap things to do for fun in big cities. Buy a cheap bottle of wine and have a nice picnic in the park. Take a long walk and explore a new neighborhood. We love visiting the dog park, playing board games, or throwing a small party at home. The key is to plan ahead for your nights and weekends. Boredom leads to spending money.

Remember your goals

This advice will not do you any good if you aren't clear about why you are saving. I know my financial independence number and that I want to reach it by age 45. I know that I need to save half to get there.

My goal is to make work optional, so I have the freedom to do what I want. More time to be creative, to make content that opens people's eyes to the power of financial literacy. Time to explore everything in this beautiful city and the independence to travel far beyond. It all comes back to goals and vision. Be clear about what you want. Know what it will take you to reach financial independence and what you'll do when you achieve it.

FINAL THOUGHTS AND TAKEAWAYS

It is possible to save half of your income, even if you live in an expensive city. First, focus on your housing and transportation costs. Live with someone else to save on rent. Consider a variety of neighborhoods and be persistent when searching for an affordable apartment that meets your needs. Don't forget to factor in transportation costs. Target areas that have good access to transit—and then use it!

To save on food and entertainment, always look for deals and discounts. Take advantage of the number of free and cheap activities that major metropolitan areas have to offer. Lastly, keep your goals front and center. Remember *why* you are working so hard to save half. What will you do when you achieve financial independence when you get to decide how to spend your time?

CHAPTER TWENTY-FIVE

How to Achieve FIRE on a Low Income

You can achieve FIRE with a modest income. Here's how…

When it comes to early retirement or the FIRE movement in general, many assume you have to be a super high earner to achieve it. However, it's a myth that all people that achieve FIRE are six-figure plus income earners. If you're on a low income and aspire to retire early, or even on time, there are practical actions and money tips you should be thinking about because anyone can retire early if they get resolved about it.

Be allergic to debt

Pretend you're literally allergic to debt. True story: I once thought I was allergic to the cold. I built a narrative up in my head about it and you should do the same when it comes to debt. You're allergic. Stay away. Debt is the enemy of financial independence and the opposite of it. If you have debt, especially bad consumer debt, you are going to have to focus nearly all of your energy on eliminating it. Chip away at these debts each week or month. Know your numbers. Know the debts inside and out and focus on the ones accruing the most interest. If you side hustle, use 100% of that side hustle income to crush your debt.

Get started early with saving and investing

Any amount helps and that's because of the power of compound interest, where the money you invest also earns money, and that new money earns more money, and so on from there. Get familiar with compound interest calculators. Run the numbers and let the math guide you because compound interest is very exciting and motivating when you first learn about it. Here's an example:

If you only ever max out a Roth IRA, that's $6,000 a year or $500 a month, and you started at age 22 with nothing, your money could be worth nearly $2 million dollars at age 65 if it earned a 7.5% rate of return on average. Best of all, IRA accounts offer a tax benefit you don't get with individual investing.

If you only *saved* $6,000 in cash a year starting at age 22, that money would only be worth $258,000 at age 65. Yes, investing it over those 43 years means your money should be worth nearly 8 times more. Powerful, right?

Develop your money mindset and money mentality

You don't have to obsess over money. If you're on a low income, money is already stressful, but be consistent. Develop an abundance mindset. Exude positivity. It's your responsibility to look out for your personal finances and your future financial success, no matter your income. Nobody is going to do it for you. In fact, everybody else wants your money. It's your job to protect it.

For the most part, they don't teach personal finance in school. To make it worse, talking about money has become taboo. The good news is there is tons of awesome free information available. If you're feeling down because of your low income trust me, you're not out. Use this as a chip on your shoulder. Consider the odds of you achieving FIRE and if you don't currently like those odds, work every day towards changing them. That's a positive money mindset.

Avoid name brands

Go generic whenever that's an option until generic can't get the job done. This means cereal, clothes, backpacks, lunch meat, and even liquor. Generic is Kirkland Signature at Costco. It's regular instead of premium gas unless your car requires it. It's H&M instead of J. Crew. I even shop for Amazon's generic clothing brand called Goodthreads and love it.

Whenever you can, make small good decisions and go generic to save. It's a great habit to build up now and as long as you're not in high school, I assure you nobody is judging you or cares. Everyone else is too busy thinking about themselves to notice your no-name casual shirt and shoes.

Bonus Tip: Stop going shopping as a social activity. If you're on a low income, you *must* find affordable social activities. Shopping with friends is the opposite of that, even if you're shopping for generic brands or a big sale. Never forget, buying something on sale isn't saving money as you are still spending it. The sooner you internalize that, the better.

Take advantage of benefits only offered to people on a low income

I'll start with a concrete example: stimulus checks in the US. There have been 3 rounds. Do you know who didn't receive anything? Individuals who earned over $120,000 annually. Even those over $80,000 were phased out quickly in the last round. There are lots of programs to look into for low-income earners. My credit union offers to cover closing costs as a grant for first-time homebuyers, but you're only eligible under your area median income.

IRAs (Individual Retirement Accounts) start to phase out around $124,000 a year. You're totally ineligible at $139,000 annual income. Also, less income means you're in a lower tax bracket which means you'll pay less in taxes. I'm not saying it pays to be a low-income earner, but there are some benefits, and way more than these, that you'll discover if you do some research.

Participate in the new "permission-less" society

A college degree no longer seems to be a prerequisite to join the middle or upper class. There are far fewer gatekeepers today than there ever have been because of the internet and the rise of the intrapreneur and online companies of one. There is no longer a singular path to achieving the American Dream. The American Dream looks far much different today than it used to. There are so many uniquely different paths to success that only a world of technology and easy-to-access free information makes possible. Our phones today are far more powerful than the first spaceship that landed on the moon.

Don't feel sorry for yourself. Feel excited about how possible anything is, for anyone that's willing to work for it. The playing field has been leveled but you need to see and understand that, and of course, take advantage of it.

The Financial Samurai

Before I finish my ten points on how to retire early, I want to share highlights from an eye-opening article called "Achieving Financial Independence on A Modest Income: $40,000 in Manhattan", by The Financial Samurai. I find it inspirational because it's a very real, honest, and vulnerable article about how someone reached financial independence with only a $40,000 salary.

Sam explained how he lived in New York on a $40,000 salary right out of college. But, because he made savings a priority, he was still able to sock away $12,000 a year. By the way, $40,000 in New York is like living on $16,500 in Austin. How did he do it? He shared a studio with a friend and that studio was only a 10-minute walk to work. They didn't have cable or internet. Work offered free food so he stayed at the office until dinner so he could get a free meal from the cafeteria.

His other big secret? He worked a *lot*. After all, staying busy is one of the best ways to save money. You literally don't have time to spend money. Plus, people spend money when they're bored. He also decided against a nice apartment since he wasn't home often. Because he wasn't home often, his utility and electricity bills were often very low. And by living close to work, he didn't spend money on transportation.

The writer also presented a more organized list of tips in the end. His tips (and my final five on the topic), from somebody that went through it, is to:

Live in a crap box

There's no reason you shouldn't continue living like a college student the first 4 or 5 years or so after college. If you didn't go to college, consider moving back in with mom and dad. It's not glamorous but you can save a *lot* and fast this way to jump-start your savings or debt payoff.

Work so much you don't have time to spend money

To add to what I've covered, do what others aren't willing to do. Put in more than 40 hours. Pursue a side hustle. Decide to get up 1 hour earlier and be productive with that hour. Read The Morning Miracle for a more productive morning. I love and recommend that book. You have to set a new bar for yourself. If you want to be different and achieve something different, it's going to take work. Think about *why* you want to achieve FIRE and keep that motivation in sight and in mind.

Don't confuse yourself with someone else

It's easy to compare yourself to the lives of others you see on social media. It will lead to a downward spiral if you continue to compare your journey to someone else's. Resist the urge, regroup, and refocus on your own goals at hand. Never try to keep up with the Joneses. Instead, learn from others who are doing things differently.

Focus on increasing your income annually with your main gig

You need to make sure your main income is going up at least 3% annually to keep up with inflation. If you're making the same money year over year, you're making less money because your money is worth less than it was before, even though it doesn't seem like it.

Eggs, bread, gas, bus fare—it's all gone up as much as 6% without you noticing it from year to year. Ask for a raise and make a point as to why you deserve it or consider looking for a different, higher-paying job. Scraping by on a low income has a fantastic long-term benefit. Once you know how to live with less because you have to, you understand you *can* live with less when you don't have to.

Once you're forced to make extreme frugal decisions, or at least good decisions constantly, you're more likely to keep making good decisions and living with less when you're making more money. Individuals who earn a lot right after high school or college never learn to be as responsible with their money as they should be. So, I know it's hard to consider when you're on a low income, but be grateful for the experience. Learn from what you're doing. Focus on good habits so that when you have more, you'll keep even more of it rather than getting better at spending it. Focus on avoiding lifestyle inflation when you do start earning more.

FINAL THOUGHTS AND TAKEAWAYS

Keep going, keep fighting, and stay positive. If you're not already, focus on becoming net worth positive and scale beyond. I dug out of a -$80,000 net worth hole in a year and a half making less than 6 figures. Financial success is the sum of small efforts repeated day in and day out. If you do this, financial success happens gradually, then suddenly.

Tips are good and great. But how the heck do you do the investing part correctly, confidently, and automatically? Let's discuss that next.

CHAPTER TWENTY-SIX

How to Invest for Long-term Wealth

Investing can be intimidating and hard. Take the simple path instead.

Investing for long-term growth is actually pretty simple. Once you have a basic understanding of compound interest and learn the difference between stocks, bonds, and index funds, investing can be stress-free, and dare I say it… fun! The best part is, you'll still outperform the vast majority of people that pick individual stocks. No tricks or gimmicks, but simple math and patience.

After listening to this episode of Bigger Pockets Money Podcast interviewing JL Collins about investing, I snagged his book The Simple Path To Wealth from the library and began re-reading it. I subscribe to JL's path and suggest you consider it as well. For the sake of brevity, I won't cover it all here, but I highly recommend checking it out if you want to know more about building long-term wealth through investing. Before we talk about what to do when investing, let's highlight a couple of no-nos:

Do NOT pick individual stocks. They can flop, and you can lose big. And you'll exhaust yourself from checking performance and fretting over every fluctuation.

Do NOT put all your investment eggs in one small basket. Instead, the best strategy is putting a bunch of eggs in one big, diverse basket and holding them for the long term.

The key is in **broad-based index funds**. As the overall market succeeds—and it will, because the market always has—you succeed.

The best part? You don't have to think about it. In terms of what to invest in, here are 3 main options I recommend:

- An index fund that tracks the entire stock market
- An index fund that tracks the S&P 500
- Total bond indexing (depending on your age and life situation)

Let's discuss each:

Invest in the Total Stock Market

Remember that whole "lots of eggs in one big, diverse basket" analogy? This is it. Buying into the total stock market gives you access to roughly 3,700 publicly traded companies in the US. This is the safe, proven approach. Index funds are the most efficient investment. Why pick all? Because *nobody* can predict which stocks will succeed in the distant future. Your best bet is to diversify and hold.

To illustrate this point of "set it and forget it," JL Collins referenced a Fidelity customer account audit that revealed the best investors are dead. The second best are the ones that forgot they had the accounts. So all of this to say: buy and hold. Keep emotions out of it. Ready to jump in on the total stock market? Consider VTSAX.

VTSAX: Vanguard Total Stock Market Index Fund Admiral Shares

This is how you buy every company in the US, roughly 3,700 publicly traded companies, and keep your ER (expense ratio) lowest. In mid-2021 it was only 0.04%. The average mutual fund ER is 1.25%. You'll pay less in fees, and you'd be VERY hard-pressed to find a fund with a lower ER.

VTSAX is the most popular broad-based index fund, and for good reason. But, if you want alternatives OR it isn't available to you, here are some low ER contenders to consider:

- SWTSX (Schwab version)

- FSKAX (Fidelity version)
- VTI (ETF version, slightly lower ER currently)

Invest in the S&P 500

S&P 500 is an index that tracks or contains the 500 largest US companies. A benefit about this index is that "losers" are phased out, and "winners" get added in every year, so growth is consistent. It automatically rebalances in your favor without you needing to do anything. You don't have to worry about what companies will succeed and which will fail. It continues that whole "set it and forget it" mentality. Invest in all 500 top companies automatically.

Ready to dip your toes in the S&P 500? Consider VFIAX.

VFIAX: Vanguard 500 Index Fund Admiral Shares

VFIAX is a great choice because VTSAX, the total US stock market, is weighted heavily towards the S&P 500 anyways. In fact, it's about 80% S&P 500. That's why the performance will be very similar. It offers slightly more risk and slightly more reward potential, but it won't drift far from the total market performance. It's an extremely solid pick, and the Vanguard ER is also 0.04%.

Want more S&P 500 options?

- SWPPX (Schwab version)
- FXAIX (Fidelity version)
- VOO (ETF version from Vanguard)

Invest in Bonds

Another egg you should consider adding to your investment basket is bonds. What are bonds? Bonds are *not* stocks. A stock is buying part ownership in a company. **When you buy bonds you are loaning money to a company or government agency.** By lending your money, you're guaranteed a return. The problem is, that return is fixed and relatively small. Think 2–3%. Not the 7–10% we've seen historically from the stock market over time, but they offer much less risk.

If you're in the wealth accumulation phase of your life (i.e. most of your working life), it is more beneficial for you to invest heavily in stocks. That's where the greatest risks, but highest rewards are. You have plenty of time for your portfolio to recover and thrive as recessions come and go. The closer you get to retirement, you can mitigate some financial risk by adding bonds to your portfolio.

Are there index funds for bonds? Yes, and once again, the total bond fund from Vanguard is top of the class. Consider VBTLX.

VBTLX: Vanguard Total Bond Index Fund

Other options include:

- SWLBX (Schwab version)
- FTBFX (Fidelity version)

Retirement Date Funds

As a bonus, I want to acknowledge target-date retirement funds because, if you have a 401(k), there's a good chance you're invested in one. They are very popular and are made up of multiple index funds. After the Pension Protection Act of 2006 was passed, many plans automatically enrolled participants in one. In a nutshell, target-date retirement funds are aggressive when you're young and become more conservative as you get older and closer to retirement (or rather the year usually indicated in the fund name).

However, they are not incredibly popular among those chasing financial independence and early retirement, as they tend to be too conservative and limit growth. To be clear, if you already have one of these, it is not a bad investment. However, it may not be optimal. They are diverse, which is great, but the fees may end up costing you. Fees act as a drag in the long run. If your 401(k) has a total stock market index fund option or an S&P 500 option, it might benefit you to pivot to that. If it's Vanguard, Schwab, or Fidelity even better.

FINAL THOUGHTS AND TAKEAWAYS

Investing for long-term growth can sound and feel intimidating. After all, investing offers risk. However, that doesn't mean there isn't a simple path. Don't let fear keep you from setting up and optimizing your investment portfolio ASAP. The longer you have money invested, the better off you will be due to the power of compound interest.

Once you spend some time setting up your simple path, it can become totally hands-off outside of a brief annual check-in to review fees and portfolio balance. Start investing, diversify your investments, buy and hold for the long term, watch out for fees, and last but not least, do your own research before investing. I am not a certified financial planner or advisor. I'm a self-proclaimed money nerd.

If your cash isn't invested because you feel intimidated, always remember:

"Done is better than perfect." -Sheryl Sandberg

or

"Simple is better than complicated." -Me

For more details about this simple path, I recommend you consider picking up a copy of JL Collins' book The Simple Path to Wealth.

CHAPTER TWENTY-SEVEN

How to Stay Motivated When You're Years from FIRE

Patience young grasshopper

On your journey to financial independence, there comes a time when more or less, you have mapped out your path. You have examined your spending and identified areas to cut. You are adhering to some kind of budget. You are saving and investing half or more of your income. You even have automated payments set up so that you don't need to think about your finances each month.

This is all great! But what's next? Essentially, it's now a waiting game. For many people, this is the most difficult part. It's the biggest hurdle they will face on their financial independence journey: impatience. It's frustrating, and it can lead you into a spiral of self-doubt. Hitting this wall could cause you to make drastic changes or even give up on your goal entirely. It can hit when you are first getting started or when you are only a few years away from your financial independence number.

Having the right mindset is a crucial aspect of your financial independence journey, and a key component of this is learning how to stay motivated when you inevitably hit a wall. By taking these five steps, you can overcome impatience and self-doubt, enabling you to stay motivated on the path to financial independence.

Internalize how compound interest works

If you are feeling stuck at the beginning of your journey, remember that compound interest is on your side. It's slow at first, then rapidly increases the longer you're invested. It's your invested assets earning money, then those earnings are reinvested, and it snowballs exponentially from there over time. If you commit to long-term investing in low-cost index funds and reinvesting dividends, you will make it mathematically more feasible to achieve FI most years.

When it comes to investment returns, momentum is everything. Beyond earnings and numbers, momentum also occurs on an emotional level. On the path to FI, tracking your net worth will help you discover momentum as you see your net worth rise. It's addicting. It's motivating. I find myself setting more challenging goals, and I achieve more financial success, almost gamifying it.

I thought net worth zero was an amazing feat in early 2019 (I started at -$80,000 in late 2017). Then I blew past $50,000. Then I achieved 6-figures. Now I'm approaching $250,000. This isn't a brag. I'm sharing to illustrate 1) The importance of tracking your net worth and 2) I've personally experienced it getting easier over time when the ball gets rolling.

Tracking your net worth will also keep you motivated but you *must* invest. You cannot reach F.I. from savings alone. It's practically impossible. The longer you invest consistently, the more exponential interest you will earn. One crucial part of this strategy is to not check your accounts daily. Ignore the ups and downs of the market. Checking your net worth too frequently will drive you crazy. As best as you can, set your investments and leave them alone. Consistently investing will lead to big rewards in the long run. Be patient and trust the process.

Keep learning and trying new things

If you are feeling discouraged as you work towards financial independence, try seeking out new information and acquiring new skills. Learning more about personal finance can keep you motivated by helping you discover new ideas to put into practice to improve your savings rate or your investment strategy. Read books or watch

YouTube videos about personal finance topics that interest you.

Keep learning in other areas of your life as well. If you feel static in your life, it's easy to feel static on your financial independence journey. If you are bored at work, it may be time to find a new job. You could also pick up a new side hustle or hobby that you have always wanted to try. Even if it costs money, throw yourself into a new activity or one that you love. This will help you get out of your head and break out of your rut.

Break down goals and celebrate small wins

Financial independence is a huge goal. Achieving your financial independence can be extremely overwhelming. It may feel impossible, especially when you are first starting. A great way to stay focused on your big goal is to break it down into small, digestible parts and celebrate when you reach these milestones.

It's important to recognize and celebrate how hard you have worked to reach each goal. Plan to do something fun whenever you max out your 401(k) or IRA, when you get a raise at work, or when you hit a certain amount of money earned from a side hustle. Enjoy a nice dinner out or splurge on a bottle of champagne to celebrate. Reward yourself with something that you enjoy, even if it's not perfectly within your budget.

Put your goals front and center

Make sure that you see your goals every day to remind yourself what you are working towards. Find quotes that inspire you. Keep your goals in sight by updating your computer or phone background or by putting a picture on your desk that will encourage you to keep pursuing your big goal. It could be a photo of your kids or partner who you want to spend more time with or the places that you want to travel to when you reach financial independence. Seeing your goals every day will remind you what you are looking forward to in early retirement and help you stay motivated to keep going.

Enjoy the journey

The most important step is to remember that the journey is the best part. When you are working towards financial independence, it's easy to get stuck living in the future. Sometimes you can feel as if you're counting down the hours until the end of the workday, the days until Friday, and the years until you can finally retire and do what you want to do each day. This is no way to live. If you are early on in your journey, don't skip ahead to forty, fifty, or sixty years old in your mind. The best thing you can do for yourself is to remember that you have so much to enjoy along the way. Your time is your most valuable resource. Appreciate life and the time that you have and practice gratitude for each day and each experience.

To summarize:

The five steps to take to stay motivated on your journey to financial independence are:

1. Understand that compound interest works slowly at first, and then quickly.
2. Always keep learning new things—in your financial journey, your work, and your life.
3. Break down your financial independence goal into smaller chunks and celebrate reaching each milestone.
4. Keep your goals in sight to remind yourself what you are working towards.
5. Enjoy the journey. Remember, it's the best part!

At the end of the day, financial independence as a mathematical goal is fairly simple. Changing your behaviors and mindset around money may take more work. Staying motivated is one of the hardest parts of changing your mindset, however, following these five steps will help you stay on the path.

Part VI

Nuts and Bolts of FIRE

CHAPTER TWENTY-EIGHT

Why FIRE Is Easier To Reach Than Ever

Let me count the ways...

When I first heard of financial independence and the FIRE movement, I remember thinking: *How is this FIRE movement stuff possible? If it's so easy, why haven't people been doing this for decades?* It never seemed tangible or possible to me. But the more I looked into it and started taking action, I quickly understood how the everyday person can achieve financial independence and retire early without major day-to-day sacrifices. I also realized FIRE is gaining popularity because it's getting easier to achieve every year.

I found success in practice, but more importantly, I found evidence in research. The facts should get you excited to get on the FI path because it's easier than most people think. Plus, it will help you develop a positive relationship with earning money, saving money, and investing money.

The reasons why financial independence is easier than ever to reach

First, we must acknowledge humans have an innate desire to make progress and improve our lives. We want better lives for ourselves, our communities, and future generations. Furthermore, in a capitalistic society, we are incentivized to create new things, solve problems, and do more with less. In doing so, we can be financially rewarded.

In recent decades we've enjoyed huge innovations and efficiencies causing trade, capitalism, and technology to boom. Companies can market to more people than ever, earn more customers than ever, and thus enjoy higher profits than ever. This has led to increased wages (though not proportionately to inflation) over time.

The data shows wages are increasing at a higher rate than inflation most years, outside of a very odd swing the other way, because 2021 refuses to be normal...

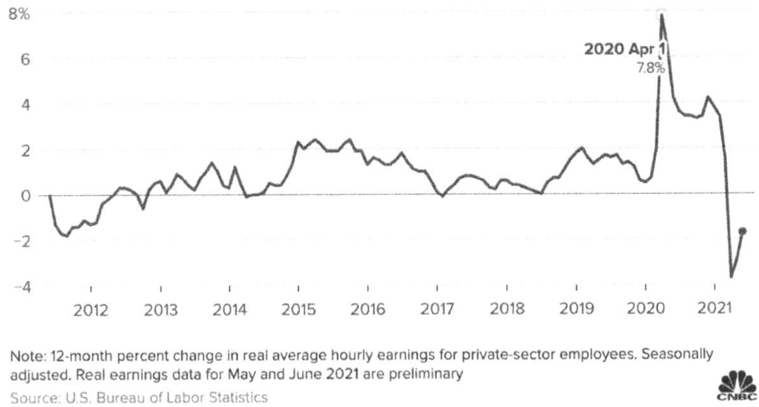

Source: CNBC

As I look at where I live, the state of Washington, our minimum wage is $13.69 an hour and on track to hit $15 by 2023. 20 years ago, it was $6.72, less than half of what it is today. Due to human innovation and incomes rising, the portion of our income used to pay for many essentials has gotten smaller over time. It has led to many smaller expenses becoming cheaper due to automation in manufacturing. Total output has increased dramatically in the last decade. That output plus innovation has pushed down costs of certain types of products—think TVs, furniture, clothing, computers, books, fast food, and more.

Transportation is most people's second-largest line item annually, but it has never been easier to live without a car or share one with a partner. We also have excellent phone apps to help us find a nearby bus or rideshare. Some argue Ubers will even get cheaper when they are automated as self-driving cars.

Additionally, it's easier than ever to live in a smaller space. For one thing, the size of the things we own has literally shrunk in many cases. We no longer own huge sound systems or bulky TVs. We no longer have bookshelves filled with encyclopedias and books, thanks to Kindle. Not to mention minimalism and clean aesthetics are trendy!

Don't people find new ways to spend money?

Yes, I fully recognize most Americans are good at spending money even when they can save money. Most aren't willing to live without a car or in a smaller place. They buy a bigger house than they need. They pay for more expensive child care. They opt for higher-quality clothes. They pay for house cleaners. They send their kids to private school and so on. FI isn't for them.

I'm not saying those are bad things to spend money on individually. But if you don't focus on increasing your savings rate, reaching FI will be difficult, despite everything I've explained so far. It may even feel more difficult. Those motivated and willing to enforce willpower will find it easier to reach FI. Not only are many smaller expenses coming down, your income ideally goes up throughout your career. If you're able to save and invest the difference, you'll enjoy compound returns.

Financial education is abundant

Access to education is the next reason FI gets easier every year. If compound interest, net worth, dividends reinvestment plans, or low-fee index funds are new terms to you, know that it's never been easier to learn them. There's never been more free content about the path to financial independence. Those on the FI path are voracious readers and consumers of content in the FI space. More and more of us are content creators like myself, publishing content consistently in books, on podcasts, blogs, and YouTube. That's because we've discovered the magic that happens when you increase your savings rate and invest consistently.

Save and invest half, retire twice as fast.

There are entire conferences and camps run by money nerds dedicated to financial education. There are even celebrities in personal finance and FIRE spaces. Searches for "financial independence" have dramatically increased in the last 10 years, as has the amount of content being made. The FIRE is clearly spreading. Corny, I know, but it's true. The community is quite large now.

Passive income

Passive income is everyone's favorite financial topic and for good reason. I've covered it several times so far. It has never been easier to generate. Technology and innovation have also made earning passive income extremely doable for anyone with access to laptops and the internet. Opportunities are endless online. The internet has truly been a game-changer for self-starting entrepreneurs or even the everyday person with an idea and willingness to see it through. Past generations also side hustled, but that resulted in exchanging time for money. If you side hustle today and focus on creating passive income streams, you can earn a disproportionate amount of income relative to the effort put in. The sooner you realize this and take action, the sooner you reach FI.

Passive income can dramatically take years off of your working life if you ensure that income will remain steady in retirement. With passive income, you may not need one million or two million dollars to retire. You need a steady income without having to put in consistent time. Of course, investing also contributes via the best form of passive income: dividends.

Geoarbitrage

Finally, technology and the pandemic have made it easier to live in cheaper cost of living areas. Geoarbitrage is keeping your big city job and income, but moving to a low cost of living area to work remotely. This can make a dramatic difference in a person's savings rate very quickly.

Moving even an hour from the city can cut your cost of living.

Moving out of the country might sound extreme, but if you commit to a low cost-of-living country or even city for 2 to 3 years and keep your big city salary, you might be able to save the equivalent of 10 to 15 years of savings back home. It's never been easier to move to an area where everything is much cheaper such as housing, gas, parking, milk and eggs, insurance, and more.

The path to FI is not completely downhill

Some of you are thinking: *FI sounds great, but it's impossible in practice…* You're not wrong. There are factors making it more difficult to achieve FI. Let me address the speed-bumps.

The reality is our big-spending categories have gotten more expensive such as health care, cars, houses, and insurance which combined make up over 60% of most people's spending. Further, we collectively continue to up our consumption year to year. Since 1973, the size of newly built homes has increased every year, while the price per square foot is about the same, so overall costs are up. Funny enough, household size numbers are decreasing, so we simply want more and more.

However, you can learn to live with less (or rather, what used to be normal) to avoid being house poor. You can even rent. I did as a 36-year-old without shame. Again, you can also live without a car or share one. Yeah, but… education prices are also rising. Yes, but these degrees are optional. If I knew then what I know now, I'd reconsider going to college altogether.

If you're already saddled with student loan debt, that's me too (thanks, graduate school!). However, FIRE showed me the power of getting out of bad consumer debt as aggressively as possible. Then I learned about investing vs. paying off lower interest debt like student loans.

I'm not saying delay paying your student loans, but financial literacy and long-term goals can help you prioritize instead of giving up because of a debt situation. I learned the power of time *in* the market, and I found investing more exciting than seeing my large debt shrink at a molasses pace. I may pivot my stance, but the bigger point is financial literacy gives you a choice.

Finally, you could argue taxes are on the rise. True. But that's nothing new. They always have been and likely always will be. If you're using taxes as an excuse to not even try, well, you're really missing out on the big picture and, again, time in the market. Also, look into tax-advantaged retirement accounts such as a Roth IRA or Traditional IRA. FIRE seekers aim to pay fewer taxes legally.

Financial independence is easier, but not easy...

I'm not arguing that reaching financial independence is easy. I'm arguing it's easier than it used to be, which I hope you find encouraging. There are reasons more and more people are not only dreaming of financial independence but actually achieving it. It's because of all of these reasons we discussed and more:

1. Technological advancements
2. Increased salaries
3. Essentials have become cheaper
4. It's easy to live without a car
5. You can live in a smaller space
6. Compound interest
7. Net worth tracking leads to mental motivation
8. FI education is abundant
9. Passive income opportunities
10. Geoarbitrage

Financial independence is more achievable than most people think. In fact, it's never been easier. Combine all of the above with buy-and-hold long-term tax-advantaged FIRE movement investing strategies and achieve *magic*. Once you get on the path, it's nearly impossible to fail.

We're pretty lucky to live in this day and age when you really think about it. I'm grateful for today and excited about a financially independent tomorrow. For me... and for you.

CHAPTER TWENTY-NINE

Stop Buying These 5 Things, Retire 5 Years Sooner

Come for the practical, stay for the not-so-obvious

Early retirement starts with the basics: being smart and frugal with your money—especially on the big categories that matter most. You probably know most people (maybe including yourself) spend too much money on the 5 things I'm going to cover, but I'm here to offer creative ideas or solutions to help you bring these common costs down or eliminate them completely.

Because a dollar saved is a dollar earned *and* a dollar earned and invested is lots of dollars. And no, I'm not coming after your lattes.

Here are the 5 things you need to stop buying if you want to retire early:

1. Bitcoin
2. Pokemon Cards
3. Birkin Bags
4. A Hollywood personal trainer
5. Mr. Beast Burgers

Let's start with Bitcoin.

Totally kidding of course... Now that I have your full attention, I'm going to tackle a much less sexy list but remember, it's the saving money part that's sexy. Let's start with a biggie. Stop buying...

Too much house

As previously mentioned, a big mistake many people make is buying *too much house,* tying up a huge portion of their net worth and monthly cash flow. According to Investopedia, the average single-family house has grown nearly three times in terms of square-footage from 983 in 1950 to 2,623 in 2018. Spending beyond your needs or means can lead to becoming "house poor," meaning you're paying too much for your house and don't have enough liquidity to pay other bills or save sufficiently. Counting on a home as an investment is risky. You should always diversify and not rely on real estate as the bulk of your net worth. After all, you can't retire on home equity alone.

Renters can rent too much house as well. Here are some quick tips for saving money as a renter:

- Always negotiate when your lease is up for renewal.
- See if you can lock in a better rate by committing to a 2-year lease.
- If you live alone and have an extra room, consider a roommate.
- Look for a new place between November and February when you'll have less competition.
- Search for photoless rentals on Craigslist. You might score a great place with no competition because of an incomplete advertisement others will ignore.

Eating out

Let me get this out of the way: *Stop going out to brunch.* I have a few spending pet peeves and this one peeves me. Breakfast is the most inexpensive meal of the day. Make some damn eggs and toast. Make bacon if you're feeling extra. Call a friend while you eat your cereal if brunch was "for the social aspect". Do anything but go out to brunch and order bottomless mimosas, please. Cook at home. Thanks.

But don't simply cook each meal at home (that can get expensive if you're following full recipes and don't have a stocked pantry). Seek out meals and portion sizes where you *know* you'll have leftovers. Then use those leftovers for future lunches and even dinner. Plan and prep and *never* go into the grocery store on an empty stomach.

Another tip is to document what you make. You'll have a handful of great ideas available to you that you can remake when planning your next grocery run. I recommend the app Kitchen Stories, especially their recipes that call for only 5 ingredients. If nothing else, set a maximum limit on eating out each month. For me, it's 2. As a bonus, you won't feel a huge amount of guilt when you do go out.

Streaming services

Do you remember the beginning of quarantine when you found yourself doing a puzzle on a Spring Sunday morning, reading for the first time in a month, and replaying old board games you already own? It seems like people already forget how much joy we all found in the little things as we tried to distract ourselves with so much unknown ahead.

Then, all of the sudden, a dozen new streaming services came out and took all of your money. You signed up because the trial was free. But you didn't cancel, did you? I get it. But pick 1 or 2 services and cut out the rest. Alternatively, do the free trials of Pluto, Shutter, BritBox, Quibi, and Cinnestream, etc. but set an alarm to cancel on your phone. (*I only made 1 of those up. Also, RIP Quibi.*)

You might have access to more than you realize. Prime Video is an obvious example. Apple is practically giving away Apple TV+ if you breathe in their general direction. You get a free year with the purchase of a new device. Plus, you can share your subscription with up to 4 "family members." Beyond streaming, consider all subscriptions you have. If you have an iPhone, there's a really easy way to see digital subscriptions you might have forgotten about. Click settings. Click on your name or iCloud profile. Click subscriptions. Click Cancel.

Lottery tickets

Never, and I mean *never* count on any form of the lottery as your financial problem-solving plan. Odds are greater that you'll get hit by a meteorite than win the Big One and you're five times more likely to get hit by lightning, twice. This one is simple but here's a pro tip: if you do like those $1 or $5 scratchers for fun from time to time *always have your tickets scanned. Even ones you deem as losers.* A few years back I kept a (small) pile of losers throughout the year and had them all checked before tossing. To my surprise, I had almost thrown away $12 in winners! And now you know my weakness...

Casinos shut down most of 2020 and life went on. Stay out of those when they reopen. Stop buying the big lottery tickets because you saw a large pot on the news. Put $20 towards your IRA instead.

Brand new cars

This is common knowledge but worth reiterating: The moment you drive a new car off the lot it loses 10% of its value. After 5 years, cars lose roughly 60% of their value. Cars last 15 to 20 years on average so let someone else take the hit on depreciation and buy used instead. You do not need a new car every 3–5 years. People in the FIRE community recommend this strategy if you must own a car: buy used, pay for it in full in cash, and stay in the $5,000 range.

If you buy from a dealer, *never* trade in your used car. It's always a rip-off. Sell private and keep some money in your pocket. If you own a car and don't use it often, rent it out on Turo, especially if you have a new car. Get some of that 10% depreciation back if you're comfortable lending it out. If you have a partner you live with and you have 2 cars between you, consider selling one and sharing the other. Finally, shop around for your gas. The convenient option is almost always the most expensive. Try the free GasBuddy app or search "gas prices" in Google Maps (yes, this actually works with decent accuracy). If you have a Costco or Sam's Club membership, hit the warehouse pumps.

FINAL THOUGHTS AND TAKEAWAYS

If you want to retire 5 years early stop buying:

1. More house than you need
2. Restaurant food and food to go
3. More streaming services and subscriptions than you need
4. Lottery Tickets
5. Brand New Cars

Make sense? Great. I'm off to stock up on eggs and mimosa fixings now…

CHAPTER THIRTY

To Retire Early, Ignore This Outdated Advice

Here are the new rules of thumb to follow instead...

Most common pieces of financial advice are okay at best. Some are outdated, some are aggravating, and some are flat-out wrong. Unfortunately, this traditional financial advice is holding many people back. Since most of us didn't learn about personal finance growing up, we got our financial know-how either from our parents or traditional rules of thumb. Unfortunately, this advice has not dated so well. There are a handful of commonly followed financial pieces of advice that I follow and here are my thoughts as to why it's bad advice and what you should do instead if you want to achieve true financial independence.

The 50–30–20 Rule of Thumb

The 50–30–20 rule means you should spend 50% of your money on needs, 30% of your money on wants, and 20% of your money should be saved. Worse but simpler advice says you should save 10% of your income. 10% is not enough. 20% is not enough, especially if all you do is "save" it. Instead, invest 30% and save 10% as a goal if you're currently saving 20%. To do so, reduce your needs and wants by 10% each. I recommend 40% on needs, 20% on wants, 40% invested. Call it the 40-20-40 rule if it helps!

If there's one thing I do like about the 50–30–20 rule, it's that it forces you to think about savings as a saving rate. In other words, it's how much you save as a percentage to how much you earn. Once you've built up your emergency fund or hit a savings goal like a downpayment on a house, then you should focus on increasing your investing.

Either way, focusing on your savings rate means you'll always increase your savings as you increase your earnings. I clearly preach saving half as a goal. I've flipped the traditional rule completely backward to 50% investing, 30% on needs, 20% on wants. In doing so, I can retire in as little as 17 years.

You should have $X amount saved by a certain age

This brings me once again to this damaging exercise I covered previously in Chapter 9. There are many resources explaining where you *should be* in terms of saving and investing by age if you want to retire on time. It can be an okay exercise in terms of benchmarking, but I don't know many people that are actually where they should be.

Seeing how far off you are can be demoralizing and make you want to give up. If you can't catch up, why even try? You clearly can never retire, right? Wrong. You can change your financial life at any age, on any income. It takes education, commitment, and hard work. It takes small efforts, day in and day out. Who's to decide where you should be at by age anyway? Personal finance is personal and looks different for everyone. We all have unique lives and circumstances.

Honestly, I feel a bit bad when I share on YouTube that my goal every year is to save half of my post-tax income. *Save and invest half, retire twice as fast,* I always say. I realize this could make others feel bad about their 0%-20% savings rate. I don't want to discourage anyone. I want to encourage you. Four years ago, my savings rate was *negative*. So, if I can do it, I know you can too.

Don't invest until you're completely out of debt

On the surface, this is a really simple rule to follow and isn't terrible advice, but there are so many kinds of debt. Instead, I would modify it to say "out of *credit card* debt." Credit card debt is right up there with the worst debt you can have. If you have credit card debt accruing interest, generally between 15–25%, pay that off before you invest. While paying off your credit card debt, I encourage you to learn about investing. This could be far more lucrative in the long term.

Here's a quick, semi-personal example. Let's talk about student loan debt vs. investing. If you have $50,000 in student loan debt accruing 5% interest, you might hesitate to invest. However, if you invest in the total stock market or an S&P 500 mutual fund, you should earn anywhere from 7–9% on average based on the last 50 years of market data to rely on.

Compounded over time with earnings and dividends reinvested, your investments should grow into a huge pot, especially if you start young. This would increase your net worth exponentially more than paying down a low-interest debt. (Note: If your interest rate is above 5%, focus on paying that off as a priority).

That said, if your debts are manageable and you have a debt payoff plan, I do recommend you contribute at least to the company match on your 401(k) while paying off your debts. It's better to invest a small amount now so you can learn by doing as opposed to putting off investing completely.

Renting is throwing away money

This is understandably a controversial one to dispute, but I'll offer food for thought. CBS News reported that from 1890–2005, "inflation-adjusted home prices rose only 103%, or less than 1% a year." Despite that, I do know that real estate can be an excellent investment. In the long run, owning a home or rental homes is a great way to scale your net worth in many cases. The problem is, people forget that your home is also an expense. I don't want to harp on the cons of ownership. Instead, I want to offer the often-forgotten financial pros of renting. While renting doesn't add to your net worth, it does:

- Give you the flexibility to move and live where you want, including areas with a cheaper cost of living.

- Provide opportunities to reduce your monthly payment by living with a partner or roommate (you can do this as an owner, but less actually do).
- Allow you to live in a neighborhood you couldn't afford to buy-in.
- Prevent you from paying out of pocket when something inevitably needs repair or needs to be replaced.

Some newer apartment complexes also have great amenities like a gym (saving you on a gym membership), an office or coworking space, a rooftop with communal areas and barbecues, dog runs, fire pits, free community events, and more. By buying, you're likely sinking most of your life savings into a downpayment, money you could have otherwise used to invest.

If buying keeps you out of the market for 5, 10, 15 years, or more, it may not be worth it as it could potentially delay retirement while you miss out on valuable years of earning compound interest.

And please, let's stop using the phrase "starter home." This is damaging because most people don't realize nearly all of the money you pay towards your mortgage the first 5 years goes to interest. If you are purchasing a home, intend to live in the house for 5 years or more to actually build some equity.

The truth is, owning and renting both have their pros and cons. You shouldn't feel shame if you rent. To buy or to rent is a very personal and individual decision, so if you're a renter, don't feel like you're falling behind your peers that are buying or disappointing your parents who tell you you're throwing away your money.

You should keep a balance on your credit card

While this one doesn't directly relate to retirement (or even early retirement), I have to bring it up because this is another damaging misconception. I have no idea where this myth comes from, but it is flat out wrong. Many people think it's good to have a balance on their credit cards because they've heard it's good for your credit score. Here are the facts: amounts owed relative to limits available make up 30% of your credit score. That's true. But the *lower* the utilization, the better.

A $0 balance across all your credit cards is best for 2 key reasons. First, it means you aren't accruing interest each month. Second, it'll help your credit score. In fact, paying down debt is one of the best and easiest ways to raise your score.

I love chasing rewards and points and use my credit cards to make most purchases. But I always pay them off in full every month. Please, if you take nothing else from this chapter, take this point away: Always pay off your credit cards in full each month.

And always remember: *the more you learn, the more you earn.* Let's pivot to advice you should be listening to. Let's discuss underrated financial advice most people overlook.

CHAPTER THIRTY-ONE

The Most Underrated Pieces of Financial Advice

Better is better than good

I learned from a podcast that 72% of Americans report that they stressed about money last week. It's the #1 reason why couples get divorced. It's hard to get good with money, especially since most people don't talk about it. Yes, there's lots of advice and rules of thumb out there. But a lot of it is the same information. It's the overrated, outdated, and unhelpful advice as we just covered. But what is often overlooked? What advice is underrated that could move the needle and help you stress *less* this week?

There's generic financial advice that helps you move forward. Then there's underrated advice that helps you leap ahead. Let's get to leaping.

Avoid iceberg spending

Iceberg spending is the spending that happens below the surface. For example, it could be a new hobby you try out that leads to a lifestyle shift and empty wallet. It's looking at entry or startup costs without thinking about the underlying costs it can lead to. And it happens in so many ways. You might buy a season pass at a mountain, but then you also end up buying a $500 new snowboard. Or you learn how to golf and spend $300 on a single driver.

This even happens on a small scale. You join a gym and buy new shoes, new workout clothes, a gym bag, a fitness tracker, pay for a trainer, and so on. When you buy a car there's gas, insurance, maintenance, registration, a security system, street parking, and possibly monthly parking you'll need to pay for as well. If you buy a house that's slightly bigger than you need and a tiny bit out of your budget, it's easy to justify it. The problem is that a bigger-than-you-planned house also has an extra bedroom and downstairs den to furnish.

That's iceberg spending. Be mindful. Take a beat and hit pause for a moment, and think about the costs below the surface.

Never take a job solely for the money

It's funny to say it's underrated to walk away from more money, but it's 100% true. If you're going to be unhappy doing something or are currently very unhappy doing what you do, consider doing something else.

Life is too short to spend 40+ hours a week doing something you don't *love*. Actually, I'll amend that. Life is too short to spend 40+ hours doing something you don't at least like. You don't have to *love* what you do. That's pretty rare. But you should at least like it. If you dread it and you always have a case of the Mondays, you're doing it wrong. Work is work. That's the truth. Otherwise, they'd call it "play" or "mild effort." Perhaps it's time you take stock of your feelings about it and your feelings about your salary.

It feels great to work hard and bring home some bacon. But perhaps next time you're eating that bacon, ask yourself: *was the effort worth it? Do I need all this bacon? Or do I want to be happier?*

One extra payment a year on your mortgage shortens the length of the loan by years

Plus, this saves you thousands in interest. It might be as simple as using your annual holiday bonus to accomplish this. Alternatively, you can employ a trick I recommend which is paying half of your mortgage every 2 weeks. If you do this, you'll end up paying 13 months spread out over 12 months without even realizing it.

Of course, one extra payment a year can be applied to any debt. You can and should employ this trick against your credit card and student loan debt as well. You could also flip this concept completely and use it to increase your savings by 12%. If you typically set aside $1,000 a month for, let's say a downpayment on a house as a goal, you can set aside $500 every 2 weeks, and you'll end up with $13,000 by year's end instead of $12,000. This is a handy hack if you get paid bi-weekly.

Take care of your physical and mental self

This one doesn't feel like it's about personal finance, but it is. You get one body and one mind in your lifetime. Treat them with care. All the money in the world in retirement is nothing if you can't enjoy it with a healthy body and mind.

The easiest way to do this is to eliminate bad habits and hold yourself accountable. Learn about the impact of your vices over the long term. Think about how healthy you feel now and how it would feel to feel even healthier. Even if it feels super far off, think about long-term care in retirement. It can be, and often is, your #1 expense in retirement. But many health issues are preventable with good care and good habits.

The physical is obvious, but I also mentioned the mental. I can't help you get good with your mental health in a sentence or two, but I will say this: you have to get your mind right before you can get your money right. Read, meditate, journal. Take a break from screens and things that distract you from your goals, *especially social media*. Best of all, get outside. It's great for the body and mind. Try to build a routine or habit for physical and mental self-improvement. Getting outside regularly can help you accomplish this.

Create an annual plan

This is not a daily or weekly budget you obsess over. I like to create my finance plan once a year at the beginning of January. I've filmed this exercise using my real income and expenses 2 years in a row. In my most recent video, I shared that you can make a copy of my exact annual planner with built-in formulas so you can create your plan as I do.

It's worth noting; you can create a yearly plan at any point in the year. You can either get organized, so you finish this year strong, or map out the next 12 months.

I learned a fun tip, which was to create a resolution (or perhaps an annual financial plan) right around your birthday. Instead of measuring your success on a January through December basis, measure your goals or plans by your age. Food for thought.

Again, snag my tracker and check out my video if you'd like to see how I filled it out because I explain it all completely (www.TheMoneyResolution.com/resources).

Participate in an ESPP if you have access to one

If you're wondering what an ESPP is, it stands for employee stock purchase plan. Investopedia explains it well:

An employee stock purchase plan is a company-run program in which participating employees can purchase company stock at a discounted price. Employees contribute to the plan through payroll deductions which build up between the offering date and the purchase date. At the purchase date, the company uses the employee's accumulated funds to purchase stock in the company on behalf of the participating employees.

These plans can be a great investment if used correctly. You get to buy stock in your own company at a discount, and it happens relatively easily with no effort after you enroll. Often people prioritize their 401(k) over the ESPP, but I recommend you don't look at your 401(k) and ESPP as either/or options if you have access to both. These are "Yes and" options. It can get pretty complex, to be honest, but if you have an ESPP option and you're not taking advantage of it, I recommend you do some research and consider it. It can be an excellent way to build capital.

Always ask for a discount

Always ask for a discount or a better price. The worst someone else can say is *no*. I'm not saying haggle and barter or waste time looking up prices from other stores so you can save 5 bucks on a price match. But you might be surprised what can happen if you ask.

Here are questions to consider asking:

- Do you have a first-time customer discount?
- Is there a free store membership I can sign up for that offers in-store discounts?
- Is there a special or promotion going on or upcoming you can tell me about?
- Do you offer discounts for students, teachers, seniors, military members? And so on…

Also, check-in with work. Sometimes workplaces offer discounts for things like your cell phone service. They might even be willing to pay for your cell phone service as a business expense. The bottom line is this: ask for a discount, *always*.

If your investment portfolio is boring, you're doing it right

Don't simply invest in brands you use and like because you find that exciting. Do that if that's what it takes for you to get started with investing. I did it too. I invested in Starbucks, Disney, Netflix, and Tesla, but it was a bumpy ride, and I kept looking at performance daily.

This reminds me of an underrated bonus tip: *Stop peeking at your investments*. This is how you start to let emotions take over instead of long-term logic.

Buy the boring stuff. Automate it. Set it and forget it. Put it mostly out of sight and out of mind. Purchase low-cost index funds that track the S&P 500 or entire stock market. Don't buy individual stocks. Buy a basket of them. Buy them all. It's boring, but it works.

Another related bonus tip: *Don't get caught up in anything trending or what the media is obsessed with.* Right now, that's NFTs. But that stands for "not f*cking touching" it. Obviously it doesn't, but "fungible" sounds contagious—and not in a good way... Keep an eye on it and do your research. But never get swept up in the latest financial fad or craze.

You are never too poor to give

It's okay to think of yourself first. Look out for *numero uno*. I get it. But don't stop there. You are so much more fortunate than you realize. Giving does so much good on so many levels—and not only for others.

Giving makes you feel connected to others. It helps you align and realize causes you want to stand for or support. It reminds you that you can help others. It helps you break away from a "me first" mentality because all of *this* (*life*), it's actually about *us*. I can promise you this: giving helps, no matter how much. Try to make it a habit. Give monthly or give even $5 a week. See if you can automate it. It feels good. It helps others. It builds good karma if you believe in that. A total win-win-win!

Become a self-taught financial expert

I include this last because if you're reading this book, especially near the end, it's very likely you're already doing this. But some of you still might need to hear this: *get off your butt and start learning and don't stop learning*. Always be learning. It's a big part of the 1% rule of money I covered.

It has never been easier to learn with the number of free resources we have. If you're too proud, too poor, or too terrified to meet with a financial advisor, learn how to DIY your money. Then reconsider seeing one when you feel more confident. Don't kind of learn or learn when it's convenient. Get resolved about it. In the beginning, it'll be tough. But stick it out until you have your first ah-hah moment. Once you have a big win, you'll find it's addicting. It was for me. Remember: the more you learn, the more you earn.

Speaking of earning and even hacks in this chapter, let's cover my favorite money hack to help you stack that cash fast! (By now you know I mean invest but that didn't rhyme...)

CHAPTER THIRTY-TWO

Starve and Stack Hack

This is my all-time favorite savings hack

Stack some cash fast with this hack. Say that 5 times fast... Using the 'Starve and Stack Method' is one of the best ways to shave off 5, 10, or even 15 years of working. Alternatively, if your goal is simply to retire on time and you feel behind, this method could really help you in your quest.

There is 1 key caveat I need to address before diving into how this method works and why it's so effective: this method *only* works if you and a partner each have an income *or* you personally have 2 or more sources of income. If neither applies to you, consider starting a side hustle so you can make this work!

For me, YouTube became a new stream of income in October 2020, and so far, every dollar I've made, I've diligently stashed away. That's a clue as to how the method works...Let's starve and stack. Or rather stack without starving...

Here's how it works

Live off of one income and save the other income completely. Again, that can be your income, a partner's income, or a second income you have.

If you want to be advanced and a totally impressive savings ninja, you would live off of the lower of the 2 and save the higher. That means a savings rate of over 50%. If you save and invest half or more of your income, you can retire in as little as 17 years—it's shockingly simple math.

You may not be getting all the comforts of living off of two salaries, like a new car or bigger-than-you-need house, but leveraging this strategy for a few years can be powerful to front-load your saving and investing. That's because time is your best friend when it comes to investing. You can enjoy compound returns for many years to come.

Let's run the numbers

Say 2 newlyweds make $60,000 and $40,000 respectively after tax. We'll call them Pam ($60,000) and Jim ($40,000).

To establish a nice nest egg, the couple would live off of Pam's salary of $60,000 and save and invest 100% of Jim's $40,000 salary. That's a 40% savings rate between them which is fantastic.

After 3 years of doing this, assuming an 8% annual rate of return, the couple would already have over $135,000. That's $15,000 more than they contributed.

Here's where it gets interesting...

Even if they stopped there and never contributed another dollar because of other financial goals like buying a house and having expensive babies, that $120,000 could turn into $291,455 10 years later. 20 years after starting to starve and stack, they would have $519,000. 30 years later, they would achieve millionaire status with $1.145 million. 40 years later? That $120,000 would be worth a tick over $2.5 million dollars. Now THAT'S a nest egg. And this couple only had to go all-in for 3 years.

If Jim and Pam were 25 when they got married and stopped starve and stack after 3 years at age 28, by age 65, this couple should be set on retirement with over $2.5 million to live off of. Imagine if that couple never stopped living off of one income and saving the other. We could be talking *bookoo* dollars. Yes, *bookoo* dollars. That's official investing jargon obviously.

But, continuing to contribute $10,000 a year could mean retiring early.

The other thing I love about the method is that it shows that if one of you lost a job and one income went away completely for any reason, you know you both could survive. It offers flexibility that one of you could quit your job if you're unhappy or want to pivot careers completely. Or one of you could take extended time off if and when kids arrive. Kids are expensive, though, so maybe get back to work. You need a break from those slobber monsters anyways.

Let's say instead this couple contributed $200,000 total over the course of 40 years through dollar-cost averaging—investing the same amount of money at a set interval. That is $5,000 a year saved and invested towards retirement.

Despite contributing $60,000 more dollars, by not front-loading it, it is in the market for less time. At the end of 40 steady years of investing, that nest egg would be worth just under $1.5 million dollars. That sounds good and great, right? Actually, that's more than a million dollars less than front-loading $120,000 over the course of 3 years.

Time is powerful. It's your best investment tool. It's time in the market that matters most.

In case you're wondering, contributing $120,000 over the course of 40 years in total, so $3,000 a year means you'd have just under $900,000. That's almost 3 times LESS than if you came up with $120,000 over the course of 3 years. Crazy, right?

These numbers illustrate the power of compound interest and why many people chasing financial independence with a partner live off of one income and save the other. It's brilliant and super simple. To take it one final step, if they lived off of Jim's income of $40,000 for 3 years and invested the other income of $60,000 each year, that $180,000 could be worth nearly $3.4 million 40 years later.

In that situation, they should be able to comfortably retire 30 years after getting married with over $1.5 million saved and invested. I highly encourage you to run the numbers using a compound interest calculator or retirement calculator. Although difficult in practice, this method is highly effective and simple.

Remember, you can do this as an individual as well if you have more than one income.

Money and early retirement are about getting time back so that you can enjoy more of your life with the people you love. This is why I chase FIRE. I'm chasing freedom.

CHAPTER THIRTY-THREE

The Worst Financial Mistakes According To Experts

Financial ignorance is far from bliss

I once came across an excellent question thread on Quora that caught my attention. The question was: *"As a financial advisor, what is the most common mistake you see people making with their personal finance?"*

There were 87 answers in total but only around a dozen answers were actually penned by financial advisors. I studied those answers and today I bring you the top financial mistakes I believe in and most agree with. The following are 10 money mistakes to avoid according to financial planners, remixed by an everyday finance nerd seeking early retirement.

Not investing early

When is the right time to get started with investing? Literally, as soon as you can. Typically, people in their 20s contribute close to the bare minimum into a 401(k) and that's it as it pertains to investing. That was definitely me. I missed out on a decade of compound interest growth and that's a big reason why I started my YouTube channel. I want to help people avoid the same mistakes.

Here's the potentially shocking math. If you did *nothing* but max out a Roth IRA at $6,000 a year since the year you turned 21, by age 41 you'd have over $300,000. By age 51 you'd have nearly $800,000. And by age 61—assuming you never touched it and earned a steady 8%

growth each year—you'd have nearly $1.8M dollars to enjoy in retirement. One. Point. Eight.

I've been studying this stuff for years and running those numbers got me to double-take. The best part with a Roth IRA is that you've already paid taxes on that $6,000 annually. That $1.8 million... it's all yours tax-free.

Imagine if you contributed $6,000 to a Roth IRA and $6,000 to your 401(k) every year. At age 51 you'd have around $1,500,000 dollars and you could comfortably retire early. I'm simplifying, as the market will have its ups and downs, but running these numbers emphasizes the importance of getting started early. If you wait until your 40s to start investing, you'll need to contribute $20,000 a year for 20 years to get to $1,000,000. Doable, but much more difficult when time isn't on your side.

Not saving enough

Only 18% of people feel confident that they have enough money saved towards retirement. Said another way, a whopping 82% of the US population is not on track to retire on time.

Let's discuss savings rates. It's the percentage of your after-tax income you set aside for Future You. It's not short-term savings for a vacation or concert tickets or a big purchase like a car. That's still spending. To encourage you though, my definition of saving could be encouraging.

Saving is anything that positively impacts your net worth. Making a payment towards your student loans or credit card is saving—or rather, any amount that goes towards the principle is saving. As an example, if you pay $400 to student loans and $200 to interest, you "saved" $200.

Investing is also saving. That includes your 401(k) or similar work-sponsored retirement account. It includes a Traditional or Roth IRA. Contributions to an FSA or HSA is saving. Then there's stashing cash away that you intend to leave alone. It's money for Future You in a bank account or a high-interest online savings account.

When you start to track your net worth, increasing your savings rate becomes a game and a goal. It's more motivating to see your net worth increase than your student loans go down a little at a time—it is for me at least.

Living on borrowed money

The average person has over $5,000 in credit card debt alone. It's a real issue and it's one most people need to address head-on and aggressively.

Nearly every US adult finds themselves in debt at one point or another whether it's a car loan, credit card debt, student loans, a mortgage, or maybe the worst of all: a check advance payday loan. It seems this is the American way.

It's obviously best to avoid debt at all costs—the only exception being the home you live in. All other debt is bad debt. If you have multiple consumer debts, paying them off should become mission-critical task #1. In order of "payoff importance" because of high interest, prioritize payday loans, credit cards, car notes, then student loans. Any other personal loans or money owed to friends and family should probably also rank towards the top.

With debt, you're robbing from Future You for current pleasures. Debt will only make it harder to save and it'll feel nearly impossible to invest to the level you should towards retirement, meaning you'll miss out on years of compound interest returns.

Not maintaining a contingency fund

We all know an emergency fund can be a lifesaver, but I want to offer my realistic perspective in terms of the exact amount of money you should have in an emergency fund based on age and life situation.

In your teenage years, make it a goal to save your first $1,000 either before you go off to college or before you turn 20. You'll probably need to do tasks for neighbors or get a part-time job.

In your 20s, aim to have a minimum of $3,000 to $5,000 saved. This is money you *will not touch* unless there's an extreme emergency. Double your number and aim for $6,000 to $10,000 if you get married.

In your 30s, aim to accumulate 3 to 6 months of expenses in case there's a job loss, home repair, or another extreme emergency. If you're married, aim for 6 months of expenses saved in cash at a minimum and 9 to 12 months if you have kids.

In your 40s, aim to have 12 to 18 months in an emergency fund (12 months with no kids, 18 months with kids). In your 50s, 12 months should do it since it's likely you won't be paying for dependents for long.

Being too pessimistic and too conservative

Some people have a negative attitude when it comes to money and investing. They think they're destined to be poor if they grew up poor. They think investing is too risky and "only for somebody else." They read a headline about the next big crash and think, *it's not worth it*.

Anybody, in any situation, can increase their net worth, grow their wealth, and enjoy life along the way if they get committed, get educated, stay positive, and take small actions day in and day out. That sentence is my mantra in a nutshell.

I believe commitment and positivity are the keys to financial success most people don't talk about. You have to commit to learning. If you do so, you'll know that the stock market goes up and down, but historically it returns around 8% a year on average. Again, with my Roth IRA example, you could become a millionaire by investing $6,000 a year by the time you hit retirement.

The best part is when you get educated, you learn investing isn't difficult, especially with the tools and fintech we have today: tax-advantaged accounts, automation, set-it-and-forget-it dividend reinvestment plans, and more. The stock market isn't risky. Not investing or not investing enough is. Get positive. Get educated. Take action. Thank yourself later.

Ignoring inflation

It's critical you keep inflation in mind as you work on your financial plan and action steps for your future. A dollar is worth much less than it used to. In fact, $40 dollars in 1985 is equivalent to the purchasing power of $101 today. Said in reverse, $100 in 1985 gets you the buying power of less than $38 in 2021, 36 years later. That's because everything gets more expensive each year—around 3% on average.

Only once since 1955 has the dollar actually become more valuable in a year and that was by less than half a percent. In other words, your dollar is worth less each and every year.

The sad reality is, it's going to require more money than most people realize to retire if you're in your 30s or especially your 20s. That's why it's critical you invest. Even if you save cash, that cash loses value every year. I recommend you run your numbers through a retirement calculator that accounts for inflation annually. I recommend the one by Bankrate.

Trying to time the market

In a perfect world, you would buy stocks or index funds when they're at their lowest point and sell them at their highest. The reality is far, far different. There's no way to time the market. Nobody can consistently do it. There are too many variables and factors that dictate the market on any given day or even any given minute. If it was easy, everybody would do it. Even those that study the market for a living will tell you it's impossible to time.

Don't try. Instead, do 1 or 2 things really right and you'll be set. What are those 1 or 2 things? The first is dollar-cost averaging. Invest a set amount at a set consistent interval, ignoring current market conditions. I don't spend any time researching or actively investing. I don't manually move money or physically place trades.

That's because second, automate your investments. I set up my Roth IRA within M1 Finance to transfer $250 every Wednesday morning to M1. Then, M1 Finance automatically invests it into my one index fund: VTI (the total stock market). I don't buy individual stocks. I buy them all at once, consistently and automatically. That's a bonus third: buy all of the stocks.

This $250 a week means I'll reach my $6,000 annual limit in 24 weeks. For the rest of the year, I'll put that same amount I'm used to seeing leave my account into savings. $115 a week gets you to your IRA max by the end of the year.

Don't try to time your investments. Invest consistently. Invest automatically. Buy all of the stocks. In 15 words, I just told you enough to be an extremely dangerous investor. Consider joining M1 Finance here. Currently, we both get $50 if you sign up. Then, find and watch my YouTube video that'll walk you through how to set it up step by step.

Being grossly underinsured

Insurance isn't sexy. I get it so I'll keep it brief. Most people have car insurance and might consider insurance for expensive toys like laptops, jewelry, or a car rental. But they don't usually consider disability insurance, life insurance, or better health insurance.

An emergency fund is great for smaller emergencies or an unexpected event like a car getting towed or a job loss, but insurance can cover everything else. A disease. Unexpected death. I said I'd be brief and I don't want to be depressing but do a roundup of your insurance and think holistically, especially if you have a family.

I have and recommend term life insurance. It can be as little as $20 a month for 20 to 30 years and your family will be covered if anything unexpected happens to you. I use and love Haven Life. I also have emergency-only pet insurance for $19 a month through Pawp and standard pet insurance for $43 a month with PetPlan.

Insurance feels like dead money but it's necessary. And don't forget to check around for better rates or cheaper policies once a year.

Lack of estate planning

I briefly mentioned the importance of creating a will in a YouTube video and a few commented and said, "*Yup, I need to do that. Thanks for the reminder.*" So here's your reminder: Get your estate in order. It's important and it's not as painful as you think. Make sure you have a will and beneficiaries decided on. Update this every two years if needed.

Make sure everything you worked hard to earn for your estate ends up in the correct hands. For example, I've heard countless stories on podcasts about divorced couples that forgot to update their estate plan after their separation and an ex-husband or ex-wife got everything instead of a current husband or wife. It's not a fun exercise but it's a critically important one.

Not writing down goals

First of all, goals aren't real unless you spend serious time reflecting on them, crafting them, and most importantly, writing them down. That means physically or more likely in a document digitally. I keep a short term goals note in my iPhone Notes app. I also keep a Google Doc with goals for the year financially and otherwise, as well as a 5-year plan for The Money Resolution, my personal education business.

How you do it is obviously up to you but I do recommend that you create short-term and long-term investment and personal finance goals. Specific is good, but make sure your goals are exciting, measurable, and challenging but feasible.

FINAL THOUGHTS AND TAKEAWAYS

Don't forget to include education as a part of your financial goals. They didn't teach us money in school so it's important you take the initiative and learn personal finance in your spare time as often as you can. As I always say: Get learned up or get left behind. Speaking of education, let's learn about millionaires to set the stage for learning how to become one to achieve early retirement.

Part VII

Two Comma Club

CHAPTER THIRTY-FOUR

I Studied Millionaires For You

Yes, you too can become an everyday millionaire next door

If you want to become a millionaire, you should study millionaires. Learn how they gained their wealth and study their behaviors so you can replicate it. I researched current millionaires and picked apart their success to determine what we should glean from it —what information we should use to inform our own actions to help us achieve the same level of financial success. If a million dollars to your name someday is a goal of yours, you're in the right place. I'll also share my own thoughts on the matter. What does the future millionaire look like? Is it harder or easier than ever to become an everyday millionaire? Hint: It's actually *much* easier.

Millionaire Statistics

Let's start with the data as the proof is in the pudding. Most of this is US-based, and I'll list sources in the end to simplify formatting.

- Roughly 8% of Americans are millionaires, and approximately 14% of U.S. households are in the millionaire club. That 8% is up from 6.2% in 2018 and only 5.8% in 2017.
- The Global Wealth Report says that the total number of millionaires in the US is 18.6 million. The US added 675,000 new millionaires from 2018 to 2019 alone and has more

millionaires than any other country.

- Bloomberg reported current projections are that 1,700 new U.S. millionaires are made every day, and by 2030, millennials are estimated to control five times as much wealth as they have now.
- According to the iconic book The Millionaire Next Door, 80% of millionaires are self-made, and only 20% inherited their millions. Roughly 80% of current millionaires are what you'd call first-generation millionaires who earned their wealth on their own.

These same statistics hold up when it comes to who's still working and who's retired.

- Only around 20% of millionaires are retired. The other 80% are still in the working force. This 80% statistic caught my attention. Would you still work if you had a net worth of over $1 million? You might think no, but millionaires actually still stress about their money, which causes them to work more
- According to Investopedia, most millionaires worry about retirement, their kids' college fund, and the mortgage like the rest of us. Those worries are greatest among new millionaires, the people who recently acquired their wealth.

Does a million dollars solve all your problems? Maybe not…

- The US millennial millionaires own an average of three properties with a real estate portfolio worth $1.4 million.
- In terms of age, the average age of the US millionaires is 62 years old. About 38% of US millionaires are over 65 years of age. 80% of current millionaires didn't reach $1 million until at least 50 years old.

If you're young, don't be in a hurry. Warren Buffett created nearly all of his wealth after age 52. Finally, here's a statistic for a little perspective:

- Becoming a millionaire in the US is no small feat globally. If you're a millionaire in US dollars, you are in the top 0.6% of wealth for the world's population.

If you have access to the internet that allows you to read this, it's likely you don't know what truly poor is. Gratitude is everything.

Behaviors

Learning about millionaires is one thing, but it's behaviors that reflect true change.

- 67% of wealthy people watch less than one hour of television daily, and 63% spend less than one hour daily surfing the internet.

As you might expect based on what I've previously said, most millionaires are the next-door variety, or what Chris Hogan calls "everyday millionaires" in his book. They're people who worked simple jobs, even teachers, who simply worked hard, lived below their means with modest homes and inexpensive cars and invested the money they didn't spend. Note that I didn't say saved. *You cannot save your way alone to millionaire status. You must invest.*

- 72% of millionaires cite 'smart investing' as a key to their success, according to a whitepaper published by the Spectrem Group.
- A study by the Harris Group, titled Survey of Affluence and Wealth, showed that these high net worth respondents save an average of 23% of their income. (I have to assume a good chunk of that 23% was invested right away).
- Half of all millionaires are self-employed or own their own business.
- In terms of education, 80% are college graduates, and only

about 18% of millionaires have master's degrees.

In the future, I suspect the "own their own business number" will rise, and the degree percentages will drop. I have nothing specific to back this up. However, a year+ of a pandemic forced a lot of people to rethink education and how they earn money. Many took to the internet in a work-from-home fashion, and some learned how to start an online business or develop a passive income stream or streams. I expect there's going to be a huge uprising of online business entrepreneurs with no college degrees.

Millionaires understand and believe they control their own destiny. Some have taken destiny into their own hands. There's been a rise of information products like ebooks, ETSY stores, and courses that are here to stay. In fact, the future of higher education could be online courses, as many have been forced to re-think if college still makes sense. Most of it has been online anyway this last year.

Key learnings

What does all of this tell us? What can we learn by researching millionaires? What else did I learn in studying millionaires? The data shows most millionaires are regular Joes who did it on their own. They're people who earn a modest income, focus on living below their means, and increasing their savings rate. They're individuals who invest regularly and often, especially in tax-advantaged retirement accounts.

A lot have a college education, but it's not a prerequisite by any means. They're self-made. They're more than likely self-taught. They believed becoming a millionaire was within their control. They were responsible for their financial success, and they knew they could achieve it. In other words, they had a positive mentality and can-do spirit. They've developed good financial habits, and that takes discipline and patience.

This all leads me to believe every one of us can strive to become a millionaire. It's more than possible. Frankly, it's never been easier, and we're about to see a rise in millionaire status that we haven't seen before.

Over the next 10 years, the percentage of millionaires in the U.S. is likely to shoot up from 8% because of inflation. But also because there are many more opportunities to earn money online as a side hustle. There's never been an abundance of free information. And investing has never been cheaper or easier. As I mentioned, people were forced to live below their means because of the pandemic. Savings rates were never higher. There's more information than ever out there, and for free. But never forget, money doesn't solve all of your problems. It's a tool to get your time and freedom back.

FINAL THOUGHTS AND TAKEAWAYS

If you're seeking millionaire status, develop a positive mental mindset. Surround yourself with positive information and focus on learning the how-tos, not the pessimistic advice or negative Nancy's like I covered in this YouTube video called "This is why bad news is so seductive."

You are the sum of what you surround yourself with. If you focus on the news that the sky is falling or get caught up in what's trending or all the rage now, you'll get distracted, and your sky will fall. You'll get emotional because money is emotional.

Garbage in, garbage out. Instead, focus on learning and surrounding yourself with positivity and useful information (like studying millionaires). If you focus on your money mindset and become a self-taught financial expert, if you implement what I call the 1% rule of money where you spend 1% of your day working on your personal finances, you too can be—no, you too will be—a millionaire next door. An everyday millionaire. You don't need to be an inventor, an athlete, or have any special skills or degrees. You can become financially independent by being you, and by making the right financial decisions day in and day out.

Study those that have succeeded before you. Surround yourself with people and information that help you in your journey, and stay focused on your future. After all, 88% of self-made millionaires read at least 30 minutes every day, so continue to focus on self-education. The naysayers don't believe in delayed gratification. But here's the truth about working hard now to enjoy it later in life: It's gratifying now to get on the path and stay on the path of success. Spending money doesn't give you gratification. Growing it does. Financial freedom, security, and time back does.

CHAPTER THIRTY-FIVE

How to Retire With 1 Million Dollars

Do it yourself and get there automatically

How can anyone retire with a $1 million nest egg in less than 10 minutes? Why $1 million? It makes for good math, it's a sexy number, and $1 million should sustain most people throughout their retirement years. It's as simple as that. Let's put the big ideas and core concepts from this book together in this chapter and build on it with the following chapters because 1+1 can equal $1,000,000 when combined. These concepts are far greater than the sum of their parts. Let's start with an investing refresher.

Can a super saver do it?

First off, let me stress one key point: you cannot save your way to $1 million dollars. You must invest your savings so your money can grow. If you were to save $1,000 a month, it would take you 83 years to save $1 million. Even if you stashed $2,000 in cash a month under your mattress, it would take you just shy of 43 years. Said another way, you would have to save $24,000 for 43 years to save your way to $1 million. So, unless you make 3 or 4 times more than the average person, you cannot *save* your way to $1 million. Instead, let's discuss investing, compound interest, and timelines. Your $1 million DIY realistic approach to retiring with $1 million starts now...

The simple investing strategy

Obviously, the earlier you start saving and investing, the better. Here's a chart from MoneyUnder30.com that shows how much you would have to save per month.

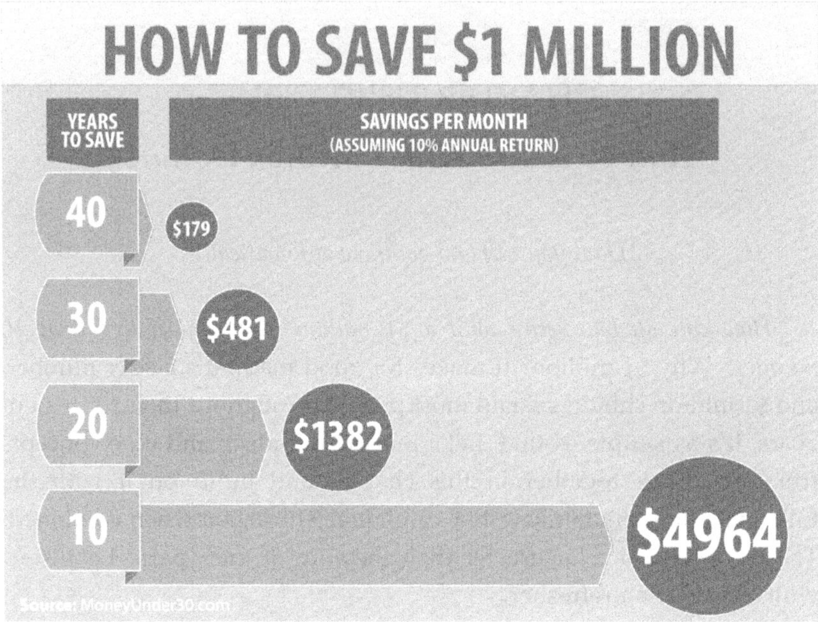

Source: MoneyUnder30.com

Assuming a 10% rate of return, which might be a bit on the high end, you would need to save only $179 a month if you have 40 years to save. $481 a month if you have 30 years. $1,382 if you have 20 years. And a whopping $4,964 over 10 years.

Notice the big jump from 10 to 20 years. That's because of the power of compound interest where your earnings also earn money, and *that* new money earns money, and so on from there. I don't want to gloss over the per month part. Consistency is key. You cannot take a month off. The best way to do this is to automate your savings and investments.

I recommend you stash money away every time you get paid or the 1st of every month. Don't leave this up to human emotion. **You**

must automate money moving from your bank account to an investment account and then into your investment fund. Doing this consistently, regardless of market performance, is a strategy called "dollar-cost averaging." I do this using M1 Finance on the days I get paid bi-weekly. I highly recommend the app.

To get to that 10% earnings, you'll need to go heavy on stocks and very light on bonds. Bonds are safe, but they typically only earn you 2 to 3%. (*Before I go on, here's your obvious "I'm not a financial advisor" disclaimer. Full disclaimer at the end. All investing includes risk.)

If you have 10 to 40 years to save, my recommendation is to go all-in on stocks. Buy a low-fee index fund that replicates the S&P 500 *or* buy the total stock market index. Don't buy individual stocks. Personally, I own 2 funds across all my portfolios: **VOO and VTI**. *My current 401(k) is an exception as it offer VTSAX as a similar equivalent.*

I did say 10% earnings might be a bit of a high assumption. But, perhaps not. We honestly don't know, and that's the point here. If you look at the S&P 500 (the top 500 stocks in the US), over the last 20 years, the average annual rate of return was around 7%.

However, if you go back further, over the last 50 years, the average annual rate of return was around 13%. Personally, I like to use 8% when making assumptions about the market and earnings.

Investing timelines and goals

That's the quick nuts and bolts of how to grow your wealth to $1 million. But how can you customize this a bit for yourself? First, you need to set your timelines.

If you're 35 now and you want to retire at 65 with $1 million saved and invested, you obviously have 30 years. Now, make your investment assumption: is it a conservative 7%? A less conservative 8%? Or a more aggressive 10%? Next, we plug our numbers into any retirement calculator you can find with a quick Google search. I use and recommend the one from Bankrate. It'll tell you exactly how much you need to save and invest each month. Then, the final but most important step is to automate the savings and automate the investing

—because cash in a brokerage account is still only cash.

That is exactly how you DIY your way to $1 million dollars much faster than you probably thought was possible. Yes, it's a bit of a simplification but simple is good.

Once you know your numbers and your goal, you can seek out more content about how to automate your savings, what brokerage account you should use (I recommend M1 Finance, but Schwab, Fidelity, and Vanguard are great as well), and what funds you want to automatically invest in each month.

Work-sponsored retirement accounts and IRAs

If you're doing this through a work-sponsored retirement account, all of this is even simpler. Usually, you only need to decide 2 things. How much you want to be taken out of each paycheck, and what you want to invest in.

Picking your funds can be a bit tricky, but I recommend a total stock market index fund from Schwab, Fidelity, or Vanguard. These tend to have the lowest fees so that your money can grow without much of a drag.

In 2021, you can contribute up to $19,500 annually through a 401(k) as a single unmarried individual. If you're over age 50, the max bumps up to $26,000. That's $1,625 a month if you're under 50 and $2,166 a month if you're over 50. Aim to max these out each year. If that max amount is less than your $1 million exercise number that we previously covered, you'll need an IRA in addition. With an IRA (Traditional or Roth), you can contribute up to $6,000 a year, which is another $500 a month.

Personally, I max out my 401(k) and invest all of it into a Fidelity S&P 500 Fund. I also max out my Roth IRA using M1 Finance to get me to $25,500 saved and invested in tax-advantaged retirement accounts.

Individual investing

You should absolutely max out any and all tax-advantaged

investing accounts before you consider investing on your own as an individual. When you invest on your own, the pro is that you don't have strict rules on limits and when you can access your money without penalty. The big con (and this is a big one!) is that your money is essentially taxed twice.

The money in your checking or savings right now was taxed when you earned it before it hit your account. Then, if you invest it, you'll pay taxes on your earnings when you take it out of the market.

If it's been in the market for less than a year, the taxes can be brutal. It's called short-term capital gains tax. It's quite a bit (up to 37% depending on your tax bracket), so if you do buy individual stocks or funds on your own, don't touch them for at least a year.

FINAL THOUGHTS AND TAKEAWAYS

First, a summary of the core ideas covered in this book and put together in this chapter:

- **Step 1:** Determine how much time you need to save $1 million between now and retirement age.
- **Step 2:** Make an assumption about the stock market. I don't recommend assuming more than an 8% return.
- **Step 3:** Use a retirement calculator to determine how much money you need to save and invest monthly.
- **Step 4:** Set up your automated saving and investing. Start with all tax-advantaged retirement accounts that are available to you. A 401(k) and IRA are most common.

Ensure that your automated cash transfer into your brokerage account is automatically invested into a fund that you prefer. Cash in a brokerage account won't grow. We did not cover this, but the same can be said for automatic dividend reinvestments. Your 401(k) will usually enroll you in a retirement date fund automatically, so you'll want to log in and change this. I suggest a fund from Fidelity, Schwab, or Vanguard that tracks the entire stock market or S&P 500 for more growth (albeit more risk, of course).

That is how you save $1 million dollars towards retirement in one lesson. This is my favorite topic to write about because growing your wealth is simpler than most people think. Now, go *stash that cash* and *invest your nest.*

CHAPTER THIRTY-SIX

How to Retire With 1 Million Dollars in 10 Years

Yes, you can become a millionaire. No, it's not complicated.

People love the idea of getting rich quickly and with little effort. And we fancy ourselves to be *way too smart* to ever fall prey to something called a "scheme". Yet, otherwise intelligent people throw money away on dumb get-rich-quick schemes all the time—from playing the lottery and buying inventory for the latest MLM, to much more nefarious scams. I'm sure I don't have to tell you all the reasons why those methods will never help you become a millionaire.

But here's what I want you to know: you can absolutely become a millionaire in a decade even if you have $0 today. It doesn't involve MLM tactics. Or lottery tickets. Or sending me your bank account info (note: never do this!). It involves hard work, creativity, and a willingness to take consistent action. It requires small efforts compounding over time.

You have to believe it's possible

This one is a bit of a prerequisite. You need a positive attitude and an open mind. If you don't have a positive attitude and courage to take action—you'll continue to do what you've always done and continue to get the same results you've always gotten.

So instead, believe that you can because you can. Journal about it. Say daily affirmations. Visualize it. Meditate on it. Create a vision board. Figure out whatever way you need to remind and encourage yourself daily that this is possible and that you are going to do it.

Break it down to realistic goals by year

Okay, the obvious way to break down your goal to a million in 10 years is to simply say: you need to save and invest $100,000 a year. Unless you're making at least $150,000 now, saving $100,000 is going to sound near impossible. So instead, let's create a path that sounds and feels more believable by weighing your income to the back half or even the final third of the 10 years.

Seems counterintuitive, doesn't it? Ah, but this is where the magic of compound interest comes in! These will be the wonder years where your money is actually working for you and not the other way around.

Here is what that path could look like:

- *Year 1: $25k*
- *Year 2: $35k*
- *Year 3: $45k*
- *Year 4: $65k*
- *Year 5: $85k*
- *Year 6: $100k*
- *Year 7: $120k*
- *Year 8: $145k*
- *Year 9: $170k*
- *Year 10: $210k*

TOTAL: $1M

Does a million feel a little more believable when you see it laid out this way? This is saving and investing $255K over the first 5 years. This means 75% of your savings and investing will happen in your second 5 years. Behold, the power of compound interest.

"But that's still so much money to save and I have $0 to start!" I hear you. Keep reading.

Increase your income

Earn more money. Great tip, I know. But hear me out on this one because there's more to it than the obvious.

There are 3 ways to earn more money:

The **1st**, easiest way to increase your income is to ask for a raise at your current job. If a raise is out of the question, consider looking for a different better paying job. Either way, you're likely leaving a lot of money on the table if you overlook this first step.

The **2nd** way to earn more money is simply to side hustle. Everyone and their mom has a side hustle these days, so ask around and see what pays best in your area, what people enjoy the most, then pick something (or a few somethings!) and try it out.

Aim to earn at least half of what you earn at work. Ideally more. Save all your side hustle earnings OR, better yet, live off your side hustle and save your entire salary.

The **3rd** and most important way to earn more money is to build a passive income stream. Passive income isn't just "earning money while you sleep." It's earning a disproportionate amount of money than you could with your time. As with side hustles, there are lots of options and tons of resources out there. Do some brainstorming and get to work building your ideal passive income stream.

Invest early and often

The earlier you learn about investing and get started the better. If you do this in your early 20s, we're not talking a million dollars in 10 years or two million in 20 years. We could be talking 3 million in 20 years. Or 5 million in your lifetime. It sounds dramatic, but it's true. In one sentence I'll give you the investing strategy I use and recommend:

Max out all of your tax-advantaged retirement accounts such as your 401(k), Roth IRA, and HSA, and invest in an index fund that tracks either the entire stock market or the S&P 500.

Buy a home and/or buy a rental property or rental properties

Many people would agree that investing in real estate is the only way to beat investing in the market in the long term. It's safe. It's steady. It's proven. If you lack the startup to invest in real estate right now, consider finding a roommate or putting your extra room on Airbnb. Squirrel away that extra income to invest in real estate. And don't think you need to be saving up for a 4 bedroom house—condos or duplexes can be incredibly profitable!

Take risks when you're young

Your 20s or even 30s is the time to start a company, invest aggressively, take a new job opportunity, or even move halfway across the world on a whim if something lucrative or exciting potentially awaits. Because if not now then when? If you don't take risks when you're young, you're very unlikely to do so when you're older. And if you take those risks when you're younger and they don't pan out, you have the time to bounce back.

Become a financial minimalist

No, I'm not saying you need to become a miserly penny-pincher or that you need to Marie Kondo everything in your life or wear the same outfits every day. I mean, you could do that and save money, but I'm talking about taking the principles of minimalism and applying them to your finances and elsewhere.

Simplify and focus on what matters most to you. Get crystal clear on your financial goals and don't let anything stand in your way. Clear out any clutter and noise that distracts you or holds you back. Get focused and repeat small efforts day in and day out. Make money. Save money. Invest money. Simplify and repeat. Most people overestimate what they can do in 1 year, but underestimate what they can do in 10 years.

What would your life look like 10 years from now if you had $1,000,000 all because you started today? What is keeping you from starting today? The answer of course is *nothing*. 10 years to become a millionaire is fantastic. But I can do you one better... let's go big and take it home!

CHAPTER THIRTY-SEVEN

How to Reach Financial Independence in 1 Year

The secret is within you

How do you achieve financial independence in one year? Can anybody do it? Yes. It's absolutely possible. And it's not complicated.

Shortly after announcing I was working on a book at the end of 2018, I told a friend my goal was to quit working my 9 to 5 in 2 years. I was going to become financially independent. I had never shared this goal with anyone and I honestly had no real idea how to get there. Living off of indie book royalties surely wasn't the ticket. 3 years later, I'm still working full time and side hustling part-time. That said, I've learned enough to be dangerous. If you're looking for the secret to retiring in 1 year, I can share *a* path and everything I've learned.

Necessary caveat: there is no silver bullet. Anyone trying to sell you is a fraud or a scammer. In order to grow, you will have to seek discomfort and be ready to discover a new path in life. It won't be easy, but if you're committed and ambitious, then there's nothing that will stop you from success.

The path

In order to reach financial independence in 1 year, you need to find a way to earn enough income passively to cover your annual expenses today and in the future. Further, the full explanation has been hiding in plain sight all along on the Financial Independence

Wikipedia page. It contains life-changing information for someone hearing and processing these ideas for the first time. It says: "If a person can generate enough income to meet their needs from sources other than their primary occupation, they have achieved financial independence regardless of age, existing wealth, or current salary."

You can choose to continue working, but you don't need to rely on occupational income once you become financially independent—where your income exceeds your expenses.

"If a 25-year-old has $100 in expenses per month, and assets that generate $100 or more per month, they have achieved financial independence. They have no need to work a regular job to pay their bills." Obviously, nobody's expenses in the US will ever be near $100 a month but this is used to prove a point that you can add 2, 3, or 10 zeroes after each of those numbers and the statement still holds true. If you earn more than you spend and can guarantee you'll continue to do so, you are officially financially independent regardless of age.

"If a 50-year-old earns $1,000,000 a month, but has expenses that equal more than that per month, they are not financially independent, as they still have to earn the difference each month to make all their payments."

I can't say it enough: to reach financial independence, you need to earn more than your expenses outside of your primary income so you no longer need to trade your time for money. If someone receives $5,000 in dividends from stocks they own, but their expenses total $4,000, they can live on their dividend income because it pays for all their expenses (dividends are cash you earn simply for being invested in dividend-paying companies. It's not usually a lot, but it's as passive as it gets). Under these circumstances, a person is financially independent. In fact, they are *extremely* financially independent—probably wealthy. It's a dream scenario, but not very realistic.

However, if this scenario was true you'd have a lot more than $5,000 invested to earn $5,000 in dividends growing and enjoying compound interest. You might be wondering, *Is dividend-investing the answer? How much would I have to have invested in dividend-paying stocks to earn $5,000 a month on average in dividends?* Someone on Quora posed this very question. One good answer gave an example covering investments in the S&P 500:

"Right now (2018), the S&P 500 has a dividend yield of about 1.89%, which means that for every $100 invested, you'll get $1.89 in dividends per year. If you want $5,000 a month, that's $60,000 per year. This works out to about $3.17 million."

In 2021, the S&P 500 dividend yield is 1.32% so you would actually need around $4.5 million. If your portfolio had a dividend yield of 3%, you'd still need $2 million invested to live off of dividends. But in a year, at any age, starting from scratch? Nearly impossible to be sure.

The Wiki goes on to say: "There are two main directions one can focus their energy: accumulating assets or reducing their expenses". I would argue the "or" should be an "and". You must accumulate assets that produce guaranteed wealth *and* reduce expenses.

Passive income

Passive income is one of the best ways to build wealth. I have 8 streams of passive income I've been working on for almost 3 years and they now cover a third of my annual spending. I earn revenue from YouTube, blogging on Medium, 3 self-published books on Amazon, audiobooks, affiliate links, my finance course, dividends from stock investments, and video sponsors. Am I doing it right? I don't know... Am I on the right track? Definitely. Do I know how you can do it *exactly*? Absolutely not. Should you copy my path? Maybe. Will it work? I don't know. You have different skills and ideas than me I'm sure. Experiment. Try. Test and learn!

Again, it starts with investing. You can earn dividends and exponentially more in growth over time because of compound interest. Beyond that, you are going to need to find a way to create something unique to your knowledge, skills, and passions—something you can deliver at scale to an audience that demands it.

The passive income equation is: your unique idea and/or thing + create demand + provide the supply (ideally digitally) = passive income. You need to create something or make something else better. This is when you have to get your creative juices flowing and think of something you can invent. Provide the answer to a real problem a select group of people have. Turn it into a digital product where inventory can be replicated at no cost to you. You can also build a business to sell.

The only way to assure this is via accumulating assets that automatically generate income, guaranteed. *Here's the passive income secret:* It's inside of you. You have to figure it out. It takes extreme determination, intense hard work, and unique skills. Put together the ingredients of determination, hard work, and skills to generate a disproportionate amount of money relative to the effort (my definition of passive income). That's the secret sauce. Is any of that easy? Not at all. Is it doable? Yes.

Leave your mark

I've always liked my 9 to 5, but I've known I was meant for more. I was meant to create and help people. Tell me if this describes you:

- You've always felt something different in your heart
- You think you were meant for more
- You want to leave a mark on the world
- You constantly wake up with new ideas and have a notebook of them
- You get lost in your creativity and daydreams and what-ifs daily

If you're nodding right now thinking, *"Yes, all of this describes me!"* You can reach financial independence in a year if you go for it and do what others are scared to try.

The roadmap is there in the definition on Wikipedia. It's also inside of you but *you must grasp it. You must take charge.* You must create something that solves a problem for a group of people. **Choose your audience. Choose your platform. Create your thing. Deliver value. Monetize it at scale.** Is it likely you'll figure all this out in a year? No. Is it possible? Yes. It's absolutely possible.

FINAL THOUGHTS AND TAKEAWAYS

STEP 1: Reduce your expenses as much as possible. Learn to live on less.

STEP 2: Figure out how to earn more than you spend annually via passive income. Start with investing. Then think and create.

Study. Get inspired. Take action. Fail. Repeat. Focus on creating something a small group of people crave. Succeed. Scale exponentially, ideally digitally. Help yourself by helping others. You are enough. You were put here for a reason. If not you, then who? If not now, then when? You can accomplish anything in life. You can accomplish a ton in a year. Yes, even achieve financial independence **regardless of age, existing wealth, or current salary.**

If you create a thing people love and want to pay you for, you will have left a mark on this world. That is more important than any amount of wealth you will accumulate in your lifetime. Reaching FI will become an afterthought. FI is a means, not an end. 3 years later I'm not financially independent, yet I'm happier than ever. On my journey, I learned FI isn't a race, nor a destination. It's a catalyst for a more rich and fulfilling life. I don't need a number saved and invested to finally feel free. Because freedom is a state of being. Money is simply a tool that gets you on the road to understanding that.

Now it's your turn. I believe in you. Get out there and kick some ass creatively, intentionally, and ethically. Your opportunity awaits. Financial freedom awaits.

Conclusion: My 21 Commandments of Personal Finance

When I was researching personal finance long-term success, I came across an excellent article called "6 Money Rules I'll Follow Until I Die". That got me thinking about my rules. So naturally, I created my own version. Then I came up with 6 more. And 6 more. And a few more after that for good measure...

I agree with the article that "everyone should have a set of money rules or financial principles that they live by." It's about finding a balance between saving for the future, and spending in the now, responsibly. These rules are clearly my own that have helped me, but I hope by sharing, you might find a few that you decide to adopt as your own. Here are my 21 personal finance commandments:

*Download a 1-sheeter with all of 21 of my commandments I have always followed, and I will always follow here.

1. I will get paid what I'm worth and spend far less than I earn.

I've never hesitated to negotiate pay or ask for what I deserve based on performance. That last part is key. Provide incredible value first and keep the conversation about your employer's needs, not your personal wants and goals. Pro tip: get the company to name figures first.

2. I will keep my housing under 25% of my income.

Some experts suggest 30%. Some say 28%. I calculated mine and it's 21% even after our recent home purchase. You too should aim to keep your housing at or below 28% at a maximum, including your utilities if you can swing it.

3. I will buy experiences, not things.

I've absolutely learned I get more happiness bang for my buck putting my money towards a concert, a trip, or even a simple picnic in a nearby park rather than some shiny new expensive toy or gadget. I haven't bought a new phone in 3 years, and I used to be the guy that bought every model on day 1 no matter what. Stuff loses value. I lose interest in stuff and sell it or give it away. Now I'm extra conscious about what I'm buying and how much enjoyment I will actually get out of it over time. When I do buy things, I go for quality over quantity.

4. I will stay 100% out of bad consumer debt.

Here's scary data to emphasize why: Only 1 in 4 millennials are debt-free, according to a 2018 Northwestern Mutual survey. 65% of Americans in debt have no idea when they'll shed it, according to The Motley Fool. The average American household has $15,654 in credit card debt and $27,669 in auto loan debt, according to the book "Financial Freedom." It gets worse… 25% of those in debt expect to die before it's paid off. Ouch. And no thanks!

5. I will marry a similarly-minded partner when it comes to money.

I learned that it's common for financial opposites to attract, so I feel personally lucky to have found a partner that values saving and living below our means as well. Bonus: I will talk openly and honestly about money with my partner, friends, and family. And apparently, people on the internet.

6. I will save half of my post-tax income—because save and invest half, retire twice as fast.

It's very difficult at first to get to a 50% savings rate. I didn't do it overnight. I first achieved this in 2019. Start at 20% and aim to increase it 5% each year until you get to 50% if you can. But don't just save. Invest. I find this is the fastest way to grow your wealth and get on the path to financial independence and freedom. You can retire in as little as 17 years if you save half.

7. I will spend on the real me—not the inauthentic version of me.

It's easy to fall into the trap of buying for the person you dream of being: an Iron Man, a Top Chef, a runway model. Or to keep up with the Joneses next door. There will always be someone who is more successful than you. There will always be someone worse off than you. Everyone has different lifestyles and goals. It benefits no one to compare yourself to others. Keep moving forward in your own personal journey, and keep learning from your victories and mistakes, one step and one day at a time.

8. I will never rely solely on one source of income.

I'm aiming to build 8 steady income sources. In videos, I broken down how I've earned over $8,000 in passive income in the first half of 2021 and my plans for the second half to double it. Give it a look if you're curious.

9. I will confidently say no.

No, I don't need extra guacamole. No, I don't need to go to bars and blow money because it's Friday night. No, I don't need the supreme car rental insurance. Or the newest TV. Or to go shopping with friends because there's a sale. No is a beautiful word. It's a million-dollar word, quite possibly literally.

10. I will always set ambitious financial goals, but I won't beat myself up if I come up short.

Saving half is a big goal. So is earning $30,000 in passive income in 2021 as a goal. I'm on track for $16,000. That's still fantastic! I also want to get to a net worth of $200,000 by the end of 2021 and $250,000 at a minimum by the end of 2022. The point is I have specific goals. Big goals. Dream big, work hard, and you will achieve success. Period.

11. I will never stop learning all things personal finance.

The more you learn, the more you earn. Plus, rules and legislation change annually. Keep up, or you might get left behind or even make a costly mistake. Not to mention, learning builds on learning and compounds, a lot like compound interest. I find 1 + 1 can equal 3 when it comes to financial literacy. I first became obsessed with YouTube to learn. Then I discovered a ton of personal finance books that opened up my eyes. I always list my 10 favorites in the description of all of my YouTube videos.

12. I will give $50 a month at a minimum.

There are so many easy ways to donate: from dropping off goods and clothes to Goodwill, to setting up a recurring $20 bi-weekly donation to a charity that means a lot to you. If you're at a place financially where you can't spare any extra money, aim to spend a few hours a month donating your time. Philanthropy is a good reminder that, while you're working on yourself, there are always people out there that are less fortunate. We can all afford to give a little. If you give a little now, you're more likely to give more later on.

13. I will follow my why of FI.

Your why of money or financial independence is like your compass. My why is freedom, flexibility, and family. Always start with the end in mind when it comes to your finances. These aren't just goals. It's the big picture. It's your dream. It's your biggest aspirations in life and it's how soon can you do it.

14. I'll be consistent and have no zero days.

This means no days off from doing something, *anything* that has to do with being responsible with my money. However, if I do miss a day or make a financial mistake, I flex to the two-day rule. If I miss a day, I can't miss two. Yes, even on the weekend, you should check your accounts, make a debt payment, side hustle, pay back a friend, and so on. *Especially* the weekend, in fact!

15. I will bank at least 90% of financial windfalls.

A windfall is new, unexpected money like a bonus from work. I literally found $10 on the ground last week at a ballgame. Instead of buying another slice of pizza or an extra beer, I put it in my pocket, where I promptly forgot about it, and it made its way home with me. That all said, if you experience a windfall and have bad consumer debt, throw 100% of it at that debt.

16. I will never lose sight of my numbers.

What doesn't get measured gets missed. I don't have a strict budget where I track every dollar. But I do have an annual planner I fill out once a year. Make a copy and use it yourself if you'd like. I track shared couple expenses, and I track my monthly passive income. These sets of numbers take very little time to update, and they keep me on track. They also help me find overcharges, unnecessary expenses, and the occasional membership or subscription I forgot to cancel.

17. I will always look for or ask for a discount.

If it's a dollar at the grocery store, I'm not clipping coupons. Otherwise, I use the plug-in Honey to help me find discount codes. I look for new customer sign-up offers. I call when the price doesn't look right. Half the time, it doesn't work, but you know what, half the time it does. Ask. You might be surprised the next time you do it.

18. I will not eat out more than once a week.

This used to be once a month, but that became too restrictive, so I adjusted to once a week. There are times where getting something affordable and healthy (yes, it does exist but is hard to find) saves you time and money. It saves you a trip to the store. It saves you cleanup. But we don't pay for delivery, and we don't get more than 1 drink. Bonus: I will bring my lunch to work every day. This is very easy while working from home. For a decade, I ate out every day for lunch. I found and eliminated this latte factor years ago, and it has easily saved me $5,000 or more since.

19. I will always own a 2-wheeler that can easily get me from A to B.

We currently share 1 car between us, and I own a Vespa. Getting my motorcycle license and that bike instead of replacing my totaled car was one of the best financial decisions I've made. That, too, has easily saved me thousands in the last few years. I'll always have it even if we have a family and decide to get a second car for any reason. It's cheaper to use daily, it's fun, and it's better for the environment. If you want all the details, watch my Vespa breakdown video. This can also be a regular bike as well for you.

20. I will aim to max out all of my tax-advantaged retirement accounts available.

That may include a 401(k), IRA, and even HSA. I will do so by investing in the total stock market. I will buy all of the stocks via a low-fee total stock market index fund. At the very least, I will invest in the top 500 consistently.

21. I will document my finance journey.

This is part of the reason I started my YouTube channel, a Medium account, and write books in the first place. Yes, I sincerely hope to help others that will listen. But I also do this for me if I can be honest. Making videos, articles, and books help me check off several commandments on this list consistently. Plus, I can't wait to look back on my work someday and rewatch the journey. To me, it's about remembering what I was learning and remembering the kind of person I was. It keeps me grounded and honest. It keeps me learning. It'll give me a laugh, I'm sure. And it helps me grow. Truthfully, deciding to start a YouTube channel and write my first book were the best decisions I've made this decade. If you're considering documenting and sharing your journey in any way, go for it!

That's the full list—my 21 finance commandments I followed in the past, the present and will follow in the future on my path for financial freedom. There's no right path or a linear path to financial freedom, but it's important to get educated and forge your own path on your personal finance journey.

Thank you for reading "Save Half, Retire Fast." I hope you learned, laughed, reflected, and got inspired. But as you know, learning and reading isn't enough. Now it's time to start or continue your journey and take action daily. Revisit this book and your favorite chapter anytime you're looking for support, advice, or a tip to push you forward. Stay resilient, stay the course, and stay positive. You can't force early retirement, but consistency is the way. Patience is a shortcut. It's how you'll discover *gradually, then suddenly* is real.

Enjoy the journey and best of luck. Always remind yourself:

If I save and invest half, I CAN retire twice as fast!

Feedback and reviews

If you'd like to get in touch, contact me at frankie@themoneyresolution.com anytime. Follow

@TheMoneyResolution on Instagram and YouTube. Plus, get 90% off my course "Save Money Resolution" at www.TheMoneyResolution.com with code SAVEHALFBOOK as my gift to you.

If you can spare a few more minutes, I would greatly appreciate a review on Amazon or GoodReads. They are tremendously important in helping other people discover the book. My deepest gratitude if you're willing to share your thoughts. I read every review and take the feedback to heart.

Appendix A: 101 Lessons I Learned About Money

I'm a list guy. I love quick lessons, tips, and hacks. I've written 2 books that each cover 101 tips and hacks so I feel uniquely qualified to write this article. I spent the last 3 years self-learning (see also: obsessing over) all things personal finance from scratch. Here are the 101 most important lessons I've learned, delivered in a no-nonsense and to the point list. It's everything I wish I knew 10 years ago. Everything I would teach my younger self if I could:

1. Pay yourself first.
2. Understand the true definition of savings: It's anything that positively increases your net worth.
3. The more you learn, the more you earn.
4. A penny saved is a penny earned.
5. Find and eliminate your latte factor or factors.
6. Ask yourself: how much is enough?
7. Financial success is small efforts, repeated day in and day out.
8. You don't need a budget. You need a why.
9. Save and invest half, retire twice as fast. If you save half of your income you can retire in as little as 17 years.
10. If you want true wealth, you must invest.
11. Don't buy individual stocks, unless it's with money you're comfortable losing 100% of.
12. Buy index funds that track the entire stock market and/or buy index funds that track the S&P 500.

13. If you're young (20s and 30s), you don't need bonds. Stick with a basket of stocks.
14. You are the sum of the 5 people you surround yourself with, financially. So choose your friends and close people carefully.
15. Make a list of financial to-do's. Circle the top 5. Don't think about the rest until the top 5 are done.
16. If you don't find a way to make money while you sleep, you'll work until you die. -Warren Buffett.
17. The best form of passive income is to create and sell information products digitally (ebooks, YouTube, courses).
18. You need a money mentor. At the very least, you need a finance hero you can study.
19. Thank your money when it comes. Thank your money when it goes.
20. If you have bad consumer debt, pay that off first before you do anything else.
21. There's no such thing as good debt.
22. Compound interest is when your money earns interest, and that money earns interest and so on from there.
23. More money doesn't mean more problems. It means more responsibilities.
24. Money doesn't buy happiness.
25. If you want to start a company, start a company of one.
26. Give, even when you feel like you have very little to give or donate. Because if you don't give money when you're broke, you're very unlikely to give when you're wealthy.
27. Giving can be giving time when you are light on funds.
28. Money, you can hack it. With creativity and my book.
29. Remember the 1% rule of money. That means to work on your personal finances for 1% of your day, which is 14:24 if we're being specific.
30. If you're buying something on sale you're not saving money. You're still spending it.
31. You need a 5 to 9.
32. Learn how to legally pay fewer taxes. Start with your tax advantage retirement accounts.

33. If you want to get good with money, get resolved about it. Set a money resolution
34. Everything you need to know about money fits on one index card.
35. Everything you need to know about early retirement fits on this downloadable index card.
36. You do not need to keep a balance on your credit cards to improve your credit score. That is a myth. The opposite is true.
37. If you *are* picking individual stocks, always bet on a winning horse.
38. You should bank 100% of your windfalls, like a bonus from work.
39. Use a tool like Personal Capital to track your net worth.
40. Build up an emergency fund before investing.
41. However much you think you need for an emergency fund, double it. Aim for 3 to 6 months of expenses in cash on hand.
42. Keep your financial goals in sight to keep them in mind.
43. Create smaller financial goals. Celebrate in a fiscally responsible way when you achieve them.
44. DO talk about money. It doesn't have to be so taboo. Especially talk about money with your partner. Literally, schedule time but don't call it a money meeting. Call it a money party.
45. Renting is awesome. You can absolutely build wealth as a renter.
46. If you are a homeowner, divide your monthly mortgage payment in half. If you get paid bi-weekly, pay that amount each paycheck. You'll pay off 13 months in 1 year.
47. If you buy your groceries online, you'll save because you won't be tempted by delicious-looking things you don't need in the store…
48. Get an HSA if you can. Invest within it. Yes, that's a thing. It provides an amazing triple tax benefit.
49. Spend your FSA or HSA savings on Amazon.
50. Don't spend money on a product that will give you the same results as an average version. Example: fancy pens vs. regular

pens to write.

51. Get 1 good travel and 1 good cashback credit card.
52. Join a warehouse club. Buy common household items in bulk.
53. Take a money health day. It's exactly what you think it is. A day off dedicated to working on your finances.
54. Get term life insurance.
55. Get pet insurance if you have a pet or pets.
56. Become a financial minimalist by consolidating investment accounts, staying organized, living on less than you earn. Keep things simple. Less is more.
57. Avoid the Diderot effect. It's when we buy nice things to match our new nice things. In other words…
58. Avoid lifestyle creep. And creeps in general.
59. Dollar-cost averaging should be your investment strategy.
60. If you have a 401(k) employer match, you *must* contribute up to the match. That's literally free money. A 100% return on your investment.
61. You can contribute to last year's IRA until you do your taxes this year.
62. Live off of 4% of your retirement investments in retirement to never run out of money (statistically speaking).
63. If you're deciding between a Traditional or Roth IRA, choose a Roth IRA. Let your money grow tax-free.
64. They didn't teach us money in school, so it's your responsibility to become a lifelong learner.
65. Save your savings in an online-only high-interest savings account. You earn next to zero interest with a big bank. That money is technically losing money year after year due to inflation.
66. Open up separate savings accounts for separate goals.
67. Sign up for a free annual credit report via www.annualcreditreport.com
68. Get money owed to you via this Today.com article that has links by state to see if money is owed to you. Think: old deposit you forgot about.
69. If you've never heard the phrase "compound interest" until

today, spend time learning about it immediately after reading this.

70. Avoid speculative investments. Yes, that includes cryptocurrency and NFTs.
71. Never gamble or buy lottery tickets. See above.
72. Your best opportunity for increasing your income is asking for a raise directly.
73. Increase your retirement saving/investing by 1% a month. You won't even notice. Future You will.
74. If you need income today, sell things around your house.
75. Challenge yourself to have a no-spend week. It's eye-opening.
76. Take time to assign beneficiaries.
77. Don't become obsessed with money.
78. File your taxes early to avoid hackers and scammers.
79. Use security management password software to avoid hackers and scammers.
80. For your clothes, find your uniform (ex: black pants and a button-up or light sweater and jeans).
81. If you can live without a car, live without a car.
82. If you can break up with your big bank, do it. Join a credit union instead.
83. Invest in yourself
84. There is at least 1 membership or subscription you can cancel. TODAY.
85. If you know nothing about investing, try robo-advisors like Betterment. Or try Acorns
86. You can only reduce your expenses by so much. But your income earning potential is unlimited.
87. If it's a purchase over $100 you're on the fence about, wait 30 days to think on it.
88. If you have to own a car, don't buy a new car.
89. When it comes to investing, understand the Rule of 72. That means taking 72 and dividing it by your expected earnings rate annually. If it's 8%: 72 divided by 8 is 9. It'll take roughly 9 years to double your money with an 8% return.
90. Your biggest opportunity to reduce your expenses is to focus

on reducing the big 3: housing, food, and transportation.

91. Credit cards are fantastic if you earn great rewards or cashback and pay them off in full each month.
92. Buy quality. Not quantity.
93. Learn to say no.
94. If you always do what you've always done, you'll always get what you've always got.
95. The 3 most important words in personal finance are automation, automation, and automation. Be sure you automate your savings.
96. Staying busy is one of the best ways to save money. Because people spend money when they're bored.
97. Don't keep up with the Joneses. Comparison is the root of unhappiness.
98. Don't look for shortcuts. Do the work.
99. The point of acquiring money is to acquire financial freedom. Also known as freedom. It's time back so you can choose how to live a more rich life. Financial freedom is a mental construct. Learn how to live rich if you aren't rich yet.
100. What would you do for work if money wasn't a factor? Consider doing that.
101. Pay it forward. A rising tide lifts all boats.

Here's a bonus: Patience is a shortcut. Slow down to enjoy the journey. It's the best part.

Appendix B: 101 Things To Do In Early Retirement

As much as I enjoy analyzing financial savings and investment paths to retirement so we can earn more time and freedom back—it often begs the question: What will you DO with all the newly found time and freedom in retirement? What can you look forward to if you're still grinding 9 to 5?

I present 101 ridiculously awesome ideas because 101 is kind of my thing. I came up with the first 80 ideas on my own in a flurry of inspiration. I found the last 20 ideas via research (they're even better than mine!). But #101 is the most valuable. You can also download the list as a PDF here.

1. Travel. Need I say more?
2. Watch the top 100 movies of all time according to IMDB.
3. Learn a handful of amazing magic tricks. Magic was my first real obsession as a kid.
4. Cook your way through an entire cookbook. Do the same with a baking cookbook.
5. Start a blog about an interest, even if it's private.
6. Support local businesses often *or* start a local business.
7. Build a fort. Because why not.
8. More specifically, build a treehouse. Someday I hope to build a Zelda-inspired-fort I saw on a YouTube video recently.
9. Adopt a street with friends. Volunteer and clean it often.
10. In general, volunteer. I recently got my vaccine and I counted

nearly 20 volunteers at one site. Amazing.

11. Start a local sports team for kids. Or become a referee or umpire.
12. Spend a week at Disney World. At least go to DisneyLand.
13. Go to the local fair. Eat all the damn scones you want.
14. Read a book, cover to cover, in one sitting.
15. Write a book. It's never been easier to self-publish a book. I've self-published 3 (so far) via Kindle Direct Publishing.
16. Watch the sunset as often as you can. Document it, especially while traveling.
17. Teach your dog a new trick or train your companion to compete in a dog competition.
18. Complete an entire coloring book. My wife recently completed a very difficult one, which is no small feat!
19. Buy and go through an entire science kit to scratch your little kid itch. Then do some more magic…
20. Write letters to friends and family and mail them. People love getting cards and letters in the mail so do that often. Bonus: write your partner love letters.
21. Speaking of, renew your vows with your partner or take a second honeymoon.
22. Reconnect with a childhood friend and/or make new friends.
23. Train for and run for a marathon.
24. Brew your own home beer. Master your recipe. Give it a ridiculous name. I'd like to make "Frank's Red Hop".
25. Master your sourdough bread recipe.
26. Take an epic road trip and/or learn how to camp "roughing it" style.
27. Start a YouTube channel for fun. YouTube is a lot of fun for me but I bet it'd be even more fun if you weren't trying to improve your metrics constantly.
28. Binge the original podcast viral hit Serial. I also suggest the first season of Startup.
29. Paint a room in your house a totally bold new color.
30. If you're single, go on a blind date.
31. Drive for Uber or Lyft, especially for the interesting

conversations with strangers.

32. Help your daughter win the girl scout cookie competition among her troup.
33. Learn how to box or take a self-defense class.
34. Paint your masterpiece. Even if it's the paint by number variety.
35. Create a positivity board. I recently did this by screenshotting positive YouTube comments and pasting them into a Google Doc.
36. Start a scrapbook or make physical photo albums. Organize family photos while you're at it.
37. Learn how to scuba dive.
38. Give your famous Ted Talk.
39. Compete in a Moth storytelling competition. Read Storyworthy first. I'm currently reading it and loving it!
40. Try your hand at standup at a local open mic.
41. Learn how to woodwork or blacksmith. I've watched a few episodes of Forged in Fire on Netflix and it's fascinating stuff.
42. Learn glass blowing or try your hand at glass art in general. Watch Blown Away on Netflix for inspiration.
43. Reorganize your storage. Take everything you don't need to Goodwill.
44. **Moves hand and in puppet voice** Learn ventriloquism.
45. Master your own barbecue or burger sauce. Bottle and sell it.
46. Update your entire wardrobe. Hint: pair back and simplify.
47. Watch all Star Wars and Marvel movies in chronological order. Bonus: rewatch all Harry Potter and Lord of the Rings movies.
48. Build a cocktail bar and work your way through a cocktail recipe book.
49. Explore a national park. Or 5.
50. Buy a second-hand guitar on Craigslist and learn how to play your favorite song. Substitute any instrument.
51. Run a 5K a day for 30 straight days.
52. Buy a boat. No, buy a used boat. Actually, restore a really run-down old boat.
53. Restore an old car. A classic. Perhaps your childhood favorite.

54. Get your motorcycle license. Take an epic motorcycle trip with a friend and read Zen and the Art of Motorcycle Maintenance. Watch my Vespa video if you want to go the scooter route.
55. Study religions that aren't your own.
56. Learn the rules of a new sport and pick a team to cheer on. I've always wanted to learn how cricket and rugby work. Plus, Seattle is getting an NHL team so I need to learn more than the basics of hockey!
57. Sell your own merchandise via print-on-demand via your own free merch store via TeeSpring.
58. Build an exotic fish tank for your house.
59. Learn a new language. Travel to a country that speaks that language as a reward for becoming fluent.
60. Buy a drone. Do epic drone stuff like drone racing.
61. Start your own home garden, especially with vegetables and herbs.
62. Read this book cover to cover that has 14,000 things to be happy about. Put a star next to your favorites.
63. Buy an outdoor portable hammock. Try to use it often.
64. Create a children's book. Listen to this podcast episode for a little inspiration. Fun fact: 81% of people think they have a book in them. Go for it!
65. Support indie authors and buy and read both of my personal finance books: The Money Resolution and/or Money, You Can Hack It.
66. Learn how to cut your own hair, if you didn't already in 2020.
67. Get on a podcast and share your story *or* start your own podcast. Who cares about the metrics. Just have fun doing it.
68. Learn 5 different ways to tie a tie and learn how to tie a bow-tie.
69. Start a vinyl record collection. Or a tie collection. Those can be loud too. Bad dad joke, sorry.
70. Get a polaroid camera and take a photo challenge. You can downloads these via ETSY.
71. Master ALL the coffee-making techniques. If you're interested in cold brew, I've been using this cold brew maker for 3 years

and love it!

72. Attend a live taping of Saturday Night Live. This will take a lot of time, energy, and resources to figure out…
73. Join a "beer league" softball team or start your own. Call your team "Over The Mound". Get it? Over the hill? The pitching mound… moving on.
74. Make your own epic Halloween costume.
75. Go all out for holiday house decorations.
76. Host Thanksgiving for the family. Do all the cooking.
77. Get your Somm certificate. Become a sommelier. Spoiler: it's very difficult.
78. Get an exotic pet. I recommend pet insurance by the way.
79. Become a substitute teacher. It's a lot easier than you probably think to get in the classroom. You can also teach from home online.
80. Rock-climb, IRL. Not the gym version.
81. Read this book (101 Things To Do In Retirement) that apparently had the same idea as me that contains 101 more awesome things you can do in retirement.
82. Get inspired by The Queen's Gambit and get really good at chess. Play in a local park against strangers.
83. Become a mentor for a neighbor, a friend's kid, a godchild, a family friend. Anyone really.
84. Get a part-time job or work as a consultant.
85. Start a Mastermind group.
86. Travel the countryside, any countryside, via train.
87. Give photography a shot, for real.
88. Pet sit or become a foster parent for a pet in need before it's forever home. Petfinder is a great resource for this.
89. Get really involved with local politics or volunteer for a campaign. Heck, run for local office.
90. Deep dive your family tree.
91. Go back to school. This could even be online. This could even be taking my course, Save Money Resolution. Get 90% off with code SAVEHALFBOOK at checkout.
92. Relocate seasonally—somewhere nice and sunny. With a pool.

And a hot tub. Bring that hammock!

93. Remodel your house or buy a fixer-upper to flip.
94. Get in the best shape of your life. I've been supplementing my workout routine with Ring Fit Adventure on the weekends and I'm loving it. It's great for all ages, seriously.
95. Become a self-taught financial guru.
96. Babysit or housesit for friends.
97. Master your impersonation skills or jokes. Put them on display on TikTok.
98. Go to open houses nearby for fun.
99. Become a bird watcher or astronomer.
100. Go make sure you have a clean bill of health from your doctor. While not awesome in and of itself, it'll help you mentally know you can do anything else on this list.
101. Make your own personal 101 things-to-do dream list. But don't call it a bucket list. That sounds too "final". Remember, retirement is only the beginning!

I always try to give bonuses and overdeliver so here are a dozen more ideas:

102. Bungee jump, skydive, or paraglide.
103. Be an extra in a movie.
104. Support local music and artists.
105. Go completely green.
106. Do random acts of kindness.
107. See a show or shows on broadway.
108. Join a book club.
109. Subscribe to The Money Resolution on YouTube and binge the videos (see: #95 above).
110. Learn to sail.
111. Learn all about meditation and mindfulness.
112. Travel the US and see a game at every MLB ballpark.
113. Invent your own game.

If anything on this list spoke to you or stood out, here's a secret:

You can do that *now*, even if you're still working a 9 to 5 or have young kids or always feel busy as long as you prioritize it. You don't have to wait until you're retired or have more time to fully live. You can make time for yourself now. Always remember that. Otherwise, enjoy your extra time in retirement. Hopefully, I helped make it at least 1% better.

Resources: YouTube Companion Videos

As mentioned in the Foreword, every chapter has a corresponding YouTube Video I've created. Watching these will help reinforce the core concepts and add to everything you've learned. Below is the full list for your viewing pleasure. You can also find all of the videos in one place via the "Save Half, Retire Fast" playlist on The Money Resolution channel. For more resources, like an annual budget planner, free course preview, 30 day challenges, and more, visit www.TheMoneyResolution.com/resources.

Foreword | I Couldn't Not Write This Book: *"The FIRE movement needs a rebrand"*
Prologue | My FIRE Story: *"Why I hated, then joined the FIRE movement"*
Introduction | Why You Should Pursue Financial Independence: *"My why of FI: The real reason you should pursue financial independence"*
Chapter 1 | Save and Invest Half, Retire Twice as Fast: *"The #1 secret to gain financial independence and retire early"*
Chapter 2 | How to Save Half of Your Income: *"How to get started with financial freedom"*
Chapter 3 | The #1 Reason People Don't Retire Early: *"The #1 hack to ensure you'll retire early"*
Chapter 4 | The 1% Rule of Money: *"The 1% rule of money - it's not what you think"*
Chapter 5 | How to Calculate Your FIRE Number: *"The 3 easy steps to calculate your financial independence number"*

Chapter 6 | Conquer This Mental Hurdle To Increase Your Savings Rate: *"How to increase your savings rate? Conquer this mental hurdle"*
Chapter 7 | Think Small to Achieve Big Savings Goals: *The secret to saving more money? Think *small* to hit big savings goals*
Chapter 8 | The Real Reason People are Bad With Money: *"The real reason people are bad with money and how to overcome it"*
Chapter 9 | You Need This Much By Age To Retire: *"How much money you need saved to retire by age... month... minute... second"*
Chapter 10 | Unexpected Ways to Gain Financial Clarity: *"7 unexpected ways to gain financial clarity"*
Chapter 11 | The Wealth Snowball: *"The Wealth Snowball - the fastest way to grow your money?"*
Chapter 12 | How to Live Rich When You're Not Rich (yet): *"7 ways to live rich when you're not rich (yet)"*
Chapter 13 | The Paradox of Wealth: *"The Paradox of Wealth: Time isn't Money, Money is Time"*
Chapter 14 | Fat FIRE vs Lean FIRE: *"Fat FIRE vs. Lean FIRE - choose your own financial freedom adventure"*
Chapter 15 | Slow FIRE vs Coast FIRE: *"Slow FI vs. Coast FI - early retirement the easy way?"*
Chapter 16 | 5 More Types of FIRE: *"Top 10 types of FIRE you need to know about"*
Chapter 17 | Financial Independence vs. Financial Freedom: *"Financial independence vs. financial freedom - this key difference changes everything"*
Chapter 18 | A Twist on the FIRE Movement Acronym: *"Why you should steal Paula Pant's version of the FIRE movement acronym"*
Chapter 19 | Is The FIRE Movement A Cult?: "Is the FIRE movement a cult?"
Chapter 20 | Myths About the FIRE Community: *"5 myths about the FIRE community - is early retirement even possible?"*
Chapter 21 | FIRE Movement Misconceptions That Need To Be Put To Bed: *"7 worst FIRE movement misconceptions that need to be put to bed"*
Chapter 22 | Is FIRE Worth It?: *"Is FIRE worth it? Early retirement downsides"*
Chapter 23 | Feeling Burnt Out? You Might Need a Mini-Retirement: *"Feeling burnt out? You might need a mini-retirement to get re-energized"*

A SPECIAL GIFT FOR YOU

SAVE MONEY RESOLUTION COURSE

Enjoy huge savings on my first online course to help you save your first (or next) $10,000 faster than you thought was positive.

You get over 2 hours of video lessons, a 15 page workbook, a personalized $10,000 blueprint, slides, and lifetime access.

Get it 90% (!) off with code SAVEHALFBOOK
as a thank you for your purchase and support!

Learn more and claim your offer at:
www.TheMoneyResolution.com

Made in the USA
Monee, IL
08 July 2025

20757115R00164